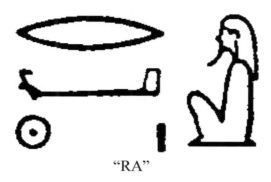

"RA"

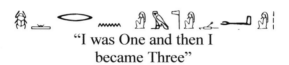

"I was One and then I
became Three"

—Ancient Egyptian Proverbs

*The Mystical Philosophy of the Priests and Priestesses of the
Ancient Egyptian City of Anu*

Fourth Edition – Expanded

Cruzian Mystic Books
P.O.Box 348
Opp, Alabama, 36467
(334) 493-8968

First U.S. edition 1997

© 1999 Second Edition By Reginald Muata Abhaya Ashby

© 2001 Third Edition By Reginald Muata Abhaya Ashby

Ashby, Muata
ANUNIAN THEOLOGY: THE MYSTERIES OF RA
ISBN: 1-884-564-38-0

Library of Congress Cataloging in Publication Data

1 Egyptian Mythology 2 Spirituality 3 Religion 4 Yoga 5 Self Help.

www.Egyptianyoga.com

**Sema
Institute of Yoga**

Sema (⚱) is an ancient Egyptian word and symbol meaning *union*. The Sema Institute is dedicated to the propagation of the universal teachings of spiritual evolution which relate to the union of humanity and the union of all things within the universe. It is a non-denominational organization which recognizes the unifying principles in all spiritual and religious systems of evolution throughout the world. Our primary goals are to provide the wisdom of ancient spiritual teachings in books, courses and other forms of communication. Secondly, to provide expert instruction and training in the various yogic disciplines including Ancient Egyptian Philosophy, Christian Gnosticism, Indian Philosophy and modern science. Thirdly, to promote world peace and Universal Love.

A primary focus of our tradition is to identify and acknowledge the yogic principles within all religions and to relate them to each other in order to promote their deeper understanding as well as to show the essential unity of purpose and the unity of all living beings and nature within the whole of existence.

The Institute is open to all who believe in the principles of peace, non-violence and spiritual emancipation regardless of sex, race, or creed.

About the author and editor:
Dr. Muata Abhaya Ashby

About The Author

Reginald Muata Ashby holds a Doctor of Philosophy Degree in Religion, and a Doctor of Divinity Degree in Holistic Healing. He is also a Pastoral Counselor and Teacher of Yoga Philosophy and Discipline. Dr. Ashby is an adjunct faculty member of the American Institute of Holistic Theology and an ordained Minister. Dr. Ashby has studied advanced Jnana, Bhakti and Kundalini Yogas under the guidance of Swami Jyotirmayananda, a world renowned Yoga Master. He has studied the mystical teachings of ancient Egypt for many years and is the creator of the Egyptian Yoga concept. He is also the founder of the Sema Institute, an organization dedicated to the propagation of the teachings of Yoga and mystical spirituality.

Dr. Ashby began his research into the spiritual philosophy of Ancient Africa (Egypt) and India and noticed correlations in the culture and arts of the two countries. This was the catalyst for a successful book series on the subject called "Egyptian Yoga". Now he has created a series of musical compositions which explore this unique area of music from ancient Egypt and its connection to world music.

Karen Clarke-Ashby "Vijaya-Asha" is the wife and spiritual partner of Muata. She is an independent researcher, practitioner and certified teacher of Yoga, a Doctor in the Sciences and a Pastoral Counselor, the editor of Egyptian Proverbs and Egyptian Yoga by Muata. ⚤

Sema Institute
P.O. Box 570459, Miami, Fla. 33257 (305) 378-6253,
Fax (305) 378-6253

Table of Contents

About the sema Institute

Sema Institute-Temple of Aset

The term "Sma" (Sema, Sama) is a derivative of the term "Smai Tawi" meaning union of the Higher and lower Self, i.e. Yoga. Thus, The Sema Institute of Yoga, Temple of Aset, founded by Dr. Muata Ashby, Seba Maa ("Seba" is a Kamitan term that means spiritual preceptor and "Maa" is an abbreviation of the word "Maat") has as its sublime goal the dissemination of the Ancient Kamitan Teachings for the upliftment of humanity through the practice and attainment of Smai Taui (Divine Union). Its primary goals are: Firstly to provide the wisdom of ancient spiritual teachings in books, courses and other forms of communication. Secondly, to provide expert instruction and training in the various yogic disciplines including Kamitan (Ancient Egyptian) Religion and Mystical Philosophy, Christian Gnosticism, Indian Mysticism which are outgrowths of Kamitan Religion. Thirdly, to promote world peace and Universal Love. As Kamitan culture, from Africa, brought forth civilization, religion and mystical philosophy to the world, a primary focus of our tradition is to identify and acknowledge the Kamitan principles within all religions and to relate them to each other in order to promote their deeper understanding and show the essential unity. In our view, Kamitan Philosophy can be the foundation for the rebuilding of African culture and bridge the gap between religious differences, which will promote harmony and peace among peoples of differing creeds and ethnic backgrounds. The Institute is open to all that believe in the principles of peace, non-violence and spiritual emancipation regardless of sex, race, or creed. The Sema Institute is an organization, which recognizes the unifying principles in all spiritual and traditions throughout the world.

"Per Aset" means Temple of Aset. In Ancient times the Temple of Aset was a mecca for all mystics, saints and sages. It was a place where the disciplines of Smai Tawi was disseminated and practiced and its influence touched Ancient Greek culture and Ancient Roman culture as well as early Christianity. The Per Aset, now based in Miami, Florida, USA, follows the rediscovered disciplines of Kamitan Smai Tawi (Yoga) and teaches these through classes, worship services and publications.

Who is Seba Muata Abhaya Ashby D.D. Ph. D.?

Priest, Author, lecturer, poet, philosopher, musician, publisher, counselor and spiritual preceptor and founder of the Sema Institute-Temple of Aset, Muata Ashby was born in Brooklyn, New York City, and grew up in the Caribbean. His family is from Puerto Rico and Barbados. Displaying an interest in ancient civilizations and the Humanities, Seba Maa began studies in the area of religion and philosophy and achieved doctorates in these areas while at the same time he began to collect his research into what would later become several books on the subject of the origins of Yoga Philosophy and practice in ancient Africa (Ancient Egypt) and also the origins of Christian Mysticism in Ancient Egypt.

Seba Maa (Muata Abhaya Ashby) holds a Doctor of Philosophy Degree in Religion, and a Doctor of Divinity Degree in Holistic Health. He is also a Pastoral Counselor and Teacher of Yoga Philosophy and Discipline. Dr. Ashby received his Doctor of Divinity Degree from and is an adjunct faculty member of the <u>American Institute of Holistic Theology</u>. Dr. Ashby is a certified as a PREP Relationship Counselor. Dr. Ashby has been an independent researcher and practitioner of Egyptian Yoga, Indian Yoga, Chinese Yoga, Buddhism and mystical psychology as well as Christian Mysticism. Dr. Ashby has engaged in Post Graduate research in advanced Jnana, Bhakti and Kundalini Yogas at the <u>Yoga Research Foundation</u>. He has extensively studied mystical religious traditions from around the world and is an accomplished lecturer, musician, artist, poet, screenwriter, playwright and author of over 25 books on Kamitan yoga and spiritual philosophy. He is an Ordained Minister and Spiritual Counselor and also the founder the Sema Institute, a non-profit organization dedicated to spreading the wisdom of Yoga and the Ancient Egyptian mystical traditions. Further, he is the spiritual leader and head priest of the Per Aset or Temple of Aset, based in Miami, Florida. Thus, as a scholar, Dr. Muata Ashby is a teacher, lecturer and researcher. However, as a spiritual leader, his title is *Seba,* which means Spiritual Preceptor.
Seba Dr. Ashby began his research into the spiritual philosophy of Ancient Africa (Egypt) and India and noticed correlations in the culture and arts of the two countries. This was the catalyst for a successful book series on the subject called "Egyptian Yoga". Now he has created a series of musical compositions which explore this unique area of music from ancient Egypt and its connection to world music.

The Creation
The god Nun pushes up the solar boat and Khep-Ra emerges in order to begin the journey of millions and millions of years. On the boat can be seen the company of gods and goddesses of Anu.

Adorations to Ra-Herakhti who's body is in the Horizon!

FORWORD

This book series focuses on the specific African religions that developed in Ancient Africa that are collectively referred to as Ancient Egyptian religion. Actually, Ancient Egyptian religion is a family of related spiritual traditions which individually comprise specific spiritual philosophies, rituals and pathways to spiritual enlightenment and spiritual evolution. In the book *THE AFRICAN ORIGINS OF CIVILIZATION, MYSTICAL RELIGION AND YOGA PHILOSOPHY*- I examined African Religion in general, and showing the common fundamental principles of most African religions. So that volume series is recommended as a companion series to this one.

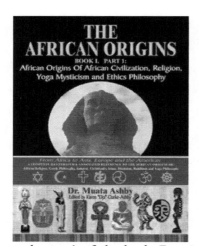

Available in one Hardcover bound volume or in three separate paperback volumes.

THE AFRICAN ORIGINS OF CIVILIZATION, MYSTICAL RELIGION AND YOGA PHILOSOPHY HARD COVER EDITION ISBN: 1-884564-50-X $80.00 U.S.   81/2" X 11"   Part 1, Part 2, Part 3 in one volume 683 Pages Hard Cover First Edition Three volumes in one. Over the past several years I have been asked to put together in one volume the most important evidences showing the correlations and common teachings between Kamitan (Ancient Egyptian) culture and religion and that of India. The questions of the history of Ancient Egypt, and the latest archeological evidences showing civilization and culture in Ancient Egypt and its spread to other countries, has intrigued many scholars as well as mystics over the years. Also, the possibility that Ancient Egyptian Priests and Priestesses migrated to Greece, India and other countries to carry on the traditions of the Ancient Egyptian Mysteries, has been speculated over the years as well. In chapter 1 of the book *Egyptian Yoga The Philosophy of Enlightenment*, 1995, I first introduced the deepest comparison between Ancient Egypt and India that had been brought forth up to that time. Now, in the year 2001 this new book, *THE AFRICAN ORIGINS OF CIVILIZATION, MYSTICAL RELIGION AND YOGA PHILOSOPHY*, more fully explores the motifs, symbols and philosophical correlations between Ancient Egyptian and Indian mysticism and clearly shows not only that Ancient Egypt and India were connected culturally but also spiritually. How does this knowledge help the spiritual aspirant? This discovery has great importance for the Yogis and mystics who follow the philosophy of Ancient Egypt and the mysticism of India. It means that India has a longer history and heritage than was previously understood. It shows that the mysteries of Ancient Egypt were essentially a yoga tradition which did not die but rather developed into the modern day systems of Yoga technology of India. It further shows that African culture developed Yoga Mysticism earlier than any other civilization in history. All of this expands our understanding of the unity of culture and the deep legacy of Yoga, which stretches into the distant past, beyond the Indus Valley civilization, the earliest known high culture in India as well as the Vedic tradition of Aryan culture. Therefore, Yoga culture and mysticism is the oldest known tradition of spiritual development and Indian mysticism is an extension of the Ancient Egyptian mysticism. By understanding the legacy which Ancient Egypt gave to India the mysticism of India is better understood and by comprehending the heritage of Indian Yoga, which is rooted in Ancient Egypt the Mysticism of Ancient Egypt is also better understood. This expanded understanding allows us to prove the underlying kinship of humanity, through the common symbols, motifs and philosophies which are not disparate and confusing teachings but in reality expressions of the same study of truth through metaphysics and mystical realization of Self. (HARD COVER)

AFRICAN ORIGINS BOOK 1 PART 1 African Origins of African Civilization, Religion, Yoga Mysticism and Ethics Philosophy-Soft Cover $24.95 ISBN: 1-884564-55-0

AFRICAN ORIGINS BOOK 2 PART 2 African Origins of Western Civilization, Religion and Philosophy(Soft) - Soft Cover $24.95 ISBN: 1-884564-56-9

EGYPT AND INDIA (AFRICAN ORIGINS BOOK 3 PART 3) African Origins of Eastern Civilization, Religion, Yoga Mysticism and Philosophy-Soft Cover $29.95 (Soft) ISBN: 1-884564-57-7

PREFACE

The Fundamental Principles of Ancient Egyptian Religion

NETERIANISM
(The Oldest Known Religion in History)

The term "Neterianism" is derived from the name "Shetaut Neter." Shetaut Neter means the "Hidden Divinity." It is the ancient philosophy and mythic spiritual culture that gave rise to the Ancient Egyptian civilization. Those who follow the spiritual path of Shetaut Neter are therefore referred to as "Neterians." The fundamental principles common to all denominations of Ancient Egyptian Religion may be summed up in four "Great Truths" that are common to all the traditions of Ancient Egyptian Religion.

Summary of Ancient Egyptian Religion

Maa Ur n Shetaut Neter

"Great Truths of The Shetaut Neter Religion"

I

Pa Neter ua ua Neberdjer m Neteru

"The Neter, the Supreme Being, is One and alone and as Neberdjer, manifesting everywhere and in all things in the form of Gods and Goddesses."

II

an-Maat swy Saui Set s-Xhemn

"Lack of righteousness brings fetters to the personality and these fetters cause ignorance of the Divine."

III

s-Uashu s-Nafu n saiu Set

"Devotion to the Divine leads to freedom from the fetters of Set."

IIII

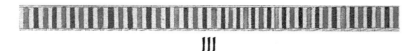

ari Shedy Rekh ab m Maakheru

"The practice of the Shedy disciplines leads to knowing oneself and the Divine. This is called being True of Speech"

Neterian Great Truths

1. ***"Pa Neter ua ua Neberdjer m Neteru"*** -"The Neter, the Supreme Being, is One and alone and as Neberdjer, manifesting everywhere and in all things in the form of Gods and Goddesses."

Neberdjer means "all-encompassing divinity," the all-inclusive, all-embracing Spirit which pervades all and who is the ultimate essence of all. This first truth unifies all the expressions of Kamitan religion.

2. **"an-Maat swy Saui Set s-Khemn"** – "Lack of righteousness brings fetters to the personality and these fetters lead to ignorance of the Divine."

When a human being acts in ways that contradict the natural order of nature, negative qualities of the mind will develop within that person's personality. These are the afflictions of Set. Set is the neteru of egoism and selfishness. The afflictions of Set include: anger, hatred, greed, lust, jealousy, envy, gluttony, dishonesty, hypocrisy, etc. So to be free from the fetters of set one must be free from the afflictions of Set.

3. **"s-Uashu s-Nafu n saiu Set"** -"Devotion to the Divine leads to freedom from the fetters of Set."

To be liberated (Nafu - freedom - to breath) from the afflictions of Set, one must be devoted to the Divine. Being devoted to the Divine means living by Maat. Maat is a way of life that is purifying to the heart and beneficial for society as it promotes virtue and order. Living by Maat means practicing Shedy (spiritual practices and disciplines).

Uashu means devotion and the classic pose of adoring the Divine is called "Dua," standing or sitting with upraised hands facing outwards towards the image of the divinity.

4. **"ari Shedy Rekh ab m Maakheru"** - "The practice of the Shedy disciplines leads to knowing oneself and the Divine. This is called being True of Speech."

Doing Shedy means to study profoundly, to penetrate the mysteries (Shetaut) and discover the nature of the Divine. There have been several practices designed by the sages of Ancient Kamit to facilitate the process of self-knowledge. These are the religious (Shetaut) traditions and the Sema (Smai) Tawi (yogic) disciplines related to them that augment the spiritual practices.

All the traditions relate the teachings of the sages by means of myths related to particular gods or goddesses. It is understood that all of these neteru are related, like brothers and sisters, having all emanated from the same source, the same Supremely Divine parent, who is neither male nor female, but encompasses the totality of the two.

The Great Truths of Neterianism are realized by means of Four Spiritual Disciplines in Three Steps

The four disciples are: Rekh Shedy (Wisdom), Ari Shedy (Righteous Action and Selfless Service), Uashu (Ushet) Shedy (Devotion) and Uaa Shedy (Meditation)

See the following page

The Three Steps are: Listening, Ritual, and Meditation

SEDJM REKH SHEDY

L I S T E N

- ***Sedjm REKH Shedy* - Listening to the WISDOM of the Neterian Traditions**

  - Shetaut Asar   – Teachings of the Asarian Tradition
  - Shetaut Anu   – Teachings of the Ra Tradition
  - Shetaut Menefer   – Teachings of the Ptah Tradition
  - Shetaut Waset   – Teachings of the Amun Tradition
  - Shetaut Netrit   – Teachings of the Goddess Tradition
  - Shetaut Aton   – Teachings of the Aton Tradition

ARI SHEDY

R I T U A L

- ***Ari Maat Shedy* – Righteous Actions – Purifies the GROSS impurities of the Heart**

  - Maat Shedy   – True Study of the Ways of hidden nature of Neter
  - Maat Aakhu   – True Deeds that lead to glory
  - Maat Aru   – True Ritual

UASHU (USHET) SHEDY

- ***Ushet Shedy* – Devotion to the Divine – Purifies the EMOTIONAL impurities of the Heart**

  - Shmai   – Divine Music
  - Sema Paut   – Meditation in motion
  - Neter Arit   – Divine Offerings – Selfless-Service – virtue -

UAA SHEDY

M E D I T A T E

- ***Uaa m Neter Shedy* -** 𓏏𓎛𓃀𓏛𓏤 **Meditation** Experience the Transcendental Supreme Self. The five forms of Neterian Meditation discipline include.

  - Arat Sekhem, -   Meditation on the Subtle Life Force
  - Ari Sma Maat, -   Meditation on the Righteous action
  - Nuk Pu-Ushet, -   Meditation on the I am
  - Nuk Ra Akhu, -   Meditation on the Glorious Light
  - Rekh – Khemn, -Meditation on the Wisdom Teaching

The Spiritual Culture and the Purpose of Life: Shetaut Neter

"Men and women are to become God-like through a life of virtue
and the cultivation of the spirit through scientific knowledge,
practice and bodily discipline."

-Ancient Egyptian Proverb

The highest forms of Joy, Peace and Contentment are obtained when the meaning of life is discovered. When the human being is in harmony with life, then it is possible to reflect and meditate upon the human condition and realize the limitations of worldly pursuits. When there is peace and harmony in life, a human being can practice any of the varied disciplines designated as Shetaut Neter to promote {his/her} evolution towards the ultimate goal of life, which Spiritual Enlightenment. Spiritual Enlightenment is the awakening of a human being to the awareness of the Transcendental essence which binds the universe and which is eternal and immutable. In this discovery is also the sobering and ecstatic realization that the human being is one with that Transcendental essence. With this realization comes great joy, peace and power to experience the fullness of life and to realize the purpose of life during the time on earth. The lotus is a symbol of Shetaut Neter, meaning the turning towards the light of truth, peace and transcendental harmony.

Shetaut Neter

We have established that the Ancient Egyptians were African peoples who lived in the north-eastern quadrant of the continent of Africa. They were descendants of the Nubians, who had themselves originated from farther south into the heart of Africa at the Great Lakes region, the sources of the Nile River. They created a vast civilization and culture earlier than any other society in known history and organized a nation that was based on the concepts of balance and order as well as spiritual enlightenment. These ancient African people called their land Kamit, and soon after developing a well-ordered society, they began to realize that the world is full of wonders, but also that life is fleeting, and that there must be something more to human existence. They developed spiritual systems that were designed to allow human beings to understand the nature of this secret being who is the essence of all Creation. They called this spiritual system "Shtaut Ntr (Shetaut Neter)."

Shetaut means secret.

Neter means Divinity.

Who is Neter in Kamitan Religion?

The symbol of Neter was described by an Ancient Kamitan priest as:
"That which is placed in the coffin"

The term Ntr ⟨⟩, or Ntjr ⟨⟩, comes from the Ancient Egyptian hieroglyphic language which did not record its vowels. However, the term survives in the Coptic language as *"Nutar."* The same Coptic meaning (divine force or sustaining power) applies in the present as it did in ancient times. It is a symbol composed of a wooden staff that was wrapped with strips of fabric, like a mummy. The strips alternate in color with yellow, green and blue. The mummy in Kamitan spirituality is understood to be the dead but resurrected Divinity. So the Nutar (Ntr) is actually every human being who does not really die, but goes to live on in a different form. Further, the resurrected spirit of every human being is that same Divinity. Phonetically, the term Nutar is related to other terms having the same meaning, such as the latin "Natura," the Spanish Naturalesa, the English "Nature" and "Nutriment", etc. In a real sense, as we will see, Natur means power manifesting as Neteru and the Neteru are the objects of creation, i.e. "nature."

Neter and the Neteru

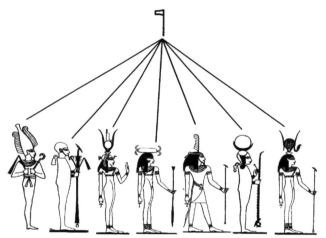

The Neteru (Gods and Goddesses) proceed from the Neter (Supreme Being)

As stated earlier, the concept of Neter and Neteru binds and ties all of the varied forms of Kamitan spirituality into one vision of the gods and goddesses all emerging from the same Supreme Being. Therefore, ultimately, Kamitan spirituality is not polytheistic, nor is it monotheistic, for it holds that the Supreme Being is more than a God or Goddess. The Supreme Being is an all-encompassing Absolute Divinity.

The Neteru

"**Neteru**"

The term "Neteru" means "gods and goddesses." This means that from the ultimate and transcendental Supreme Being, "Neter," come the Neteru. There are countless Neteru. So from the one come the many. These Neteru are cosmic forces that pervade the universe. They are the means by which Neter sustains Creation and manifests through it. So Neterianism is a monotheistic polytheism. The one Supreme Being expresses as many gods and goddesses. At the end of time, after their work of sustaining Creation is finished, these gods and goddesses are again absorbed back into the Supreme Being.

All of the spiritual systems of Ancient Egypt (Kamit) have one essential aspect that is common to all; they all hold that there is a Supreme Being (Neter) who manifests in a multiplicity of ways through nature, the Neteru. Like sunrays, the Neteru emanate from the Divine; they are its manifestations. So by studying the Neteru we learn about and are led to discover their source, the Neter, and with this discovery we are enlightened. The Neteru may be depicted anthropomorphically or zoomorphically in accordance with the teaching about Neter that is being conveyed through them.

Sacred Scriptures of Shetaut Neter

The following scriptures represent the foundational scriptures of Kamitan culture. They may be divided into three categories: *Mythic Scriptures*, *Mystical Philosophy* and *Ritual Scriptures*, and *Wisdom Scriptures* (Didactic Literature).

MYTHIC SCRIPTURES Literature	Mystical (Ritual) Philosophy Literature	Wisdom Texts Literature
SHETAUT ASAR-ASET-HERU The Myth of Asar, Aset and Heru (Asarian Resurrection Theology) - Predynastic **SHETAUT ATUM-RA** Anunian Theology Predynastic **Shetaut Net/Aset/Hetheru** Saitian Theology – Goddess Spirituality Predynastic **SHETAUT PTAH** Memphite Theology Predynastic **Shetaut Amun** Theban Theology Predynastic	**Coffin Texts** (C. 2040 B.C.E.-1786 B.C.E.) **Papyrus Texts** (C. 1580 B.C.E.- Roman Period)[1] Books of Coming Forth By Day Example of famous papyri: Papyrus of Any Papyrus of Hunefer Papyrus of Kenna Greenfield Papyrus, Etc.	**Wisdom Texts** (C. 3,000 B.C.E. – PTOLEMAIC PERIOD) Precepts of Ptahotep Instructions of Any Instructions of Amenemope. Etc. **Maat Declarations** Literature (All Periods) Blind Harpers Songs

---

[1] After 1570 B.C.E they would evolve into a more unified text, the Egyptian Book of the Dead.

The Neteru and Their Temples

Diagram 1: The Ancient Egyptian Temple Network

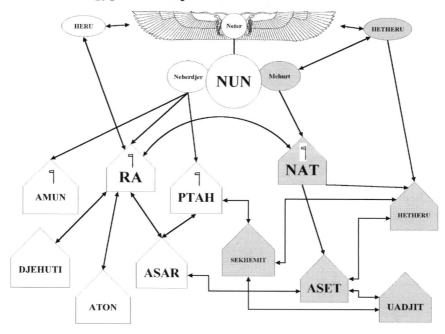

The sages of Kamit instituted a system by which the teachings of spirituality were espoused through a Temple organization. The major divinities were assigned to a particular city. That divinity or group of divinities became the "patron" divinity or divinities of that city. Also, the Priests and Priestesses of that Temple were in charge of seeing to the welfare of the people in that district as well as maintaining the traditions and disciplines of the traditions based on the particular divinity being worshipped. So the original concept of "Neter" became elaborated through the "theologies" of the various traditions. A dynamic expression of the teachings emerged, which though maintaining the integrity of the teachings, expressed nuances of variation in perspective on the teachings to suit the needs of varying kinds of personalities of the people of different locales.

In the diagram above, the primary or main divinities are denoted by the Neter symbol ( ). The house structure represents the Temple for that particular divinity. The interconnections with the other Temples are based on original scriptural statements espoused by the Temples that linked the divinities of their Temple with the other divinities. So this means that the divinities should be viewed not as separate entities operating independently, but rather as family members who are in the same "business" together, i.e. the enlightenment of society, albeit through variations in form of worship, name, form (expression of the Divinity), etc. Ultimately, all the divinities are referred to as Neteru and they are all said to be emanations from the ultimate and Supreme Being. Thus, the teaching from any of the Temples leads to an understanding of the others, and these all lead back to the source, the highest Divinity. Thus, the teaching within any of the Temple systems would lead to the attainment of spiritual enlightenment, the Great Awakening.

The Neteru and Their Interrelationships

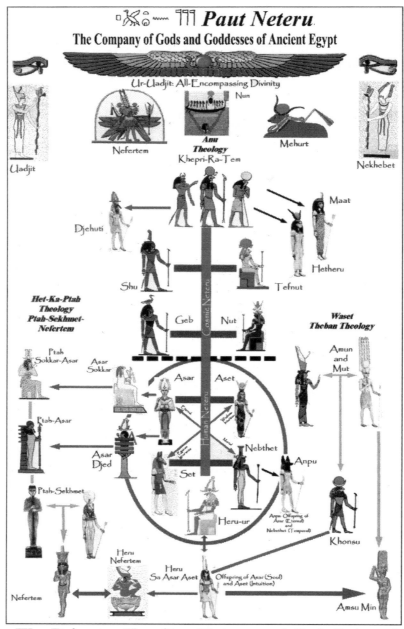

Diagram : The Primary Kamitan Neteru and their Interrelationships

The same Supreme Being, Neter, is the winged all-encompassing transcendental Divinity, the Spirit who, in the early history, is called "Heru." The physical universe in which the Heru lives is called "Hetheru" or the "house of Heru." This divinity (Heru) is also the Nun or primeval substratum from which all matter is composed. The various divinities and the material universe are composed from this primeval substratum. Neter is actually androgynous and Heru, the Spirit, is related as a male aspect of that androgyny. However, Heru in the androgynous aspect, gives rise to the solar principle and this is seen in both the male and female divinities.

The image above provides an idea of the relationships between the divinities of the three main Neterian spiritual systems (traditions): Anunian Theology, Wasetian (Theban) Theology and Het-Ka-Ptah (Memphite) Theology. The traditions are composed of companies or groups of gods and goddesses. Their actions, teachings and interactions with each other and with human beings provide insight into their nature as well as that of human existence and Creation itself. The lines indicate direct scriptural relationships and the labels also indicate that some divinities from one system are the same in others, with only a name change. Again, this is attested to by the scriptures themselves in direct statements, like those found in the ***Prt m Hru*** text Chapter 4 (17).[2]

Listening to the Teachings

"*Mestchert*"

"Listening, to fill the ears, listen attentively-"

What should the ears be filled with?

The sages of Shetaut Neter enjoined that a Shemsu Neter (follower of Neter, an initiate or aspirant) should listen to the WISDOM of the Neterian Traditions. These are the myth related to the gods and goddesses containing the basic understanding of who they are, what they represent, how they relate human beings and to the Supreme Being. The myths allow us to be connected to the Divine.

An aspirant may choose any one of the 5 main Neterian Traditions.

- Shetaut Anu — Teachings of the Ra Tradition
- Shetaut Menefer — Teachings of the Ptah Tradition
- Shetaut Waset — Teachings of the Amun Tradition
- Shetaut Netrit — Teachings of the Goddess Tradition
- Shetaut Asar — Teachings of the Asarian Tradition
- Shetaut Aton — Teachings of the Aton Tradition

---

[2] See the book *The Egyptian Book of the Dead* by Muata Ashby

The Anunian Tradition

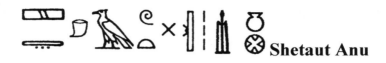 **Shetaut Anu**

The Mystery Teachings of the Anunian Tradition are related to the Divinity Ra and his company of Gods and Goddesses.[3] This Temple and its related Temples espouse the teachings of Creation, human origins and the path to spiritual enlightenment by means of the Supreme Being in the form of the god Ra. It tells of how Ra emerged from a primeval ocean and how human beings were created from his tears. The gods and goddesses, who are his children, go to form the elements of nature and the cosmic forces that maintain nature.

Below: The Heliopolitan Cosmogony.

The city of Anu (Amun-Ra)

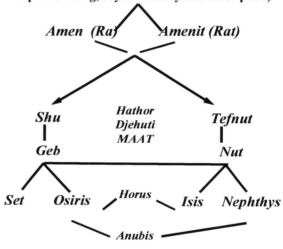

The Neters of Creation -
The Company of the Gods and Goddesses.
Neter Neteru
Nebertcher - Amun (unseen, hidden, ever present, Supreme Being, beyond duality and description)

Amen (Ra)   *Amenit (Rat)*

Shu   *Hathor Djehuti MAAT*   *Tefnut*
Geb   *Nut*

Set   *Osiris*   *Horus*   *Isis*   *Nephthys*
Anubis

Top: Ra. From left to right, starting at the bottom level- The Gods and Goddesses of Anunian Theology: Shu, Tefnut, Nut, Geb, Aset, Asar, Set, Nebthet and Heru-Ur

---

[3] See the Book Anunian Theology by Muata Ashby

The Memphite Tradition

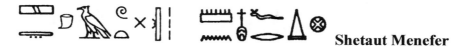 **Shetaut Menefer**

The Mystery Teachings of the Menefer (Memphite) Tradition are related to the Neterus known as Ptah, Sekhmit, Nefertem. The myths and philosophy of these divinities constitutes Memphite Theology.[4] This temple and its related temples espoused the teachings of Creation, human origins and the path to spiritual enlightenment by means of the Supreme Being in the form of the god Ptah and his family, who compose the Memphite Trinity. It tells of how Ptah emerged from a primeval ocean and how he created the universe by his will and the power of thought (mind). The gods and goddesses who are his thoughts, go to form the elements of nature and the cosmic forces that maintain nature. His spouse, Sekhmit has a powerful temple system of her own that is related to the Memphite teaching. The same is true for his son Nefertem.

Below: The Memphite Cosmogony.

The city of Hetkaptah (Ptah)

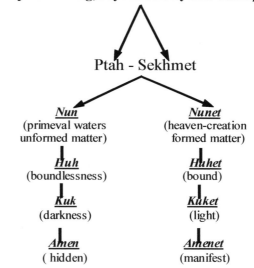

The Neters of Creation -
The Company of the Gods and Goddesses.
Neter Neteru
Nebertcher - Amun (unseen, hidden, ever present, Supreme Being, beyond duality and description)

Ptah - Sekhmet

Nun
(primeval waters unformed matter)

Nunet
(heaven-creation formed matter)

Huh
(boundlessness)

Huhet
(bound)

Kuk
(darkness)

Kuket
(light)

Amen
(hidden)

Amenet
(manifest)

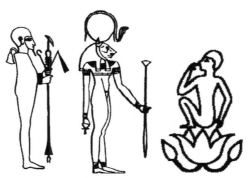

Ptah, Sekhmit and Nefertem

---

[4] See the Book Memphite Theology by Muata Ashby

The Theban Tradition

 **Shetaut Amun**

The Mystery Teachings of the Wasetian Tradition are related to the Neterus known as Amun, Mut Khonsu. This temple and its related temples espoused the teachings of Creation, human origins and the path to spiritual enlightenment by means of the Supreme Being in the form of the god Amun or Amun-Ra. It tells of how Amun and his family, the Trinity of Amun, Mut and Khonsu, manage the Universe along with his Company of Gods and Goddesses. This Temple became very important in the early part of the New Kingdom Era.

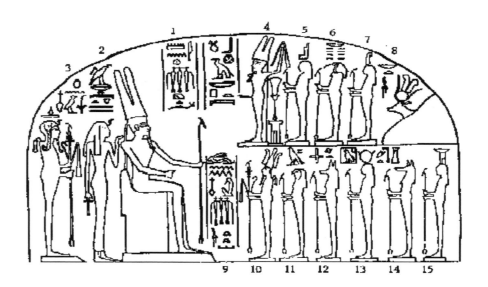

Below: The Trinity of Amun and the Company of Gods and Goddesses of Amun

See the Book *Egyptian Yoga Vol. 2* for more on Amun, Mut and Khonsu by Muata Ashby

The Goddess Tradition

Shetaut Netrit

"Arat"

The hieroglyphic sign Arat means "Goddess." General, throughout ancient Kamit, the Mystery Teachings of the Goddess Tradition are related to the Divinity in the form of the Goddess. The Goddess was an integral part of all the Neterian traditions but special temples also developed around the worship of certain particular Goddesses who were also regarded as Supreme Beings in their own right. Thus as in other African religions, the goddess as well as the female gender were respected and elevated as the male divinities. The Goddess was also the author of Creation, giving birth to it as a great Cow. The following are the most important forms of the goddess.[5]

Aset, Net, Sekhmit, Mut, Hetheru

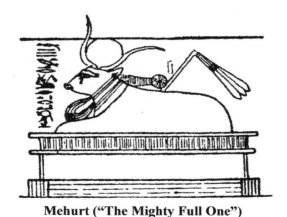

Mehurt ("The Mighty Full One")

---

[5] See the Books, *The Goddess Path, Mysteries of Isis, Glorious Light Meditation, Memphite Theology* and *Resurrecting Osiris* by Muata Ashby

The Asarian Tradition

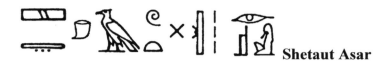 **Shetaut Asar**

This temple and its related temples espoused the teachings of Creation, human origins and the path to spiritual enlightenment by means of the Supreme Being in the form of the god Asar. It tells of how Asar and his family, the Trinity of Asar, Aset and Heru, manage the Universe and lead human beings to spiritual enlightenment and the resurrection of the soul. This Temple and its teaching were very important from the Pre-Dynastic era down to the Christian period. The Mystery Teachings of the Asarian Tradition are related to the Neterus known as: Asar, Aset, Heru (Osiris, Isis and Horus)

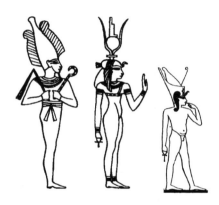

The tradition of Asar, Aset and Heru was practiced generally throughout the land of ancient Kamit. The centers of this tradition were the city of Abdu containing the Great Temple of Asar, the city of Pilak containing the Great Temple of Aset[6] and Edfu containing the Ggreat Temple of Heru.

---

[6] See the Book Resurrecting Osiris by Muata Ashby

The **Aton** Tradition

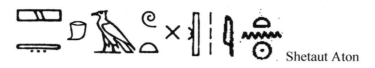 Shetaut Aton

This temple and its related temples espoused the teachings of Creation, human origins and the path to spiritual enlightenment by means of the Supreme Being in the form of the god Aton. It tells of how Aton with its dynamic life force created and sustains Creation. By recognizing Aton as the very substratum of all existence, human beings engage in devotional exercises and rituals and the study of the Hymns containing the wisdom teachings of Aton explaining that Aton manages the Universe and leads human beings to spiritual enlightenment and eternal life for the soul. This Temple and its teaching were very important in the middle New Kingdom Period. The Mystery Teachings of the Aton Tradition are related to the Neter Aton and its main exponent was the Sage King Akhnaton, who is depicted below with his family adoring the sundisk, symbol of the Aton.

Akhnaton, Nefertiti and Daughters

For more on Atonism and the Aton Theology see the Essence of Atonism Lecture Series by Sebai Muata Ashby ©2001

The General Principles of Shetaut Neter
(Teachings Presented in the Kamitan scriptures)

1. The Purpose of Life is to Attain the Great Awakening-Enlightenment-Know thyself.

2. SHETAUT NETER enjoins the Shedy (spiritual investigation) as the highest endeavor of life.

3. SHETAUT NETER enjoins that it is the responsibility of every human being to promote order and truth.

4. SHETAUT NETER enjoins the performance of Selfless Service to family, community and humanity.

5. SHETAUT NETER enjoins the Protection of nature.

6. SHETAUT NETER enjoins the Protection of the weak and oppressed.

7. SHETAUT NETER enjoins the Caring for hungry.

8. SHETAUT NETER enjoins the Caring for homeless.

9. SHETAUT NETER enjoins the equality for all people.

10. SHETAUT NETER enjoins the equality between men and women.

11. SHETAUT NETER enjoins the justice for all.

12. SHETAUT NETER enjoins the sharing of resources.

13. SHETAUT NETER enjoins the protection and proper raising of children.

14. SHETAUT NETER enjoins the movement towards balance and peace.

The Forces of Entropy

In Neterian religion, there is no concept of "evil" as is conceptualized in Western Culture. Rather, it is understood that the forces of entropy are constantly working in nature to bring that which has been constructed by human hands to their original natural state. The serpent Apep (Apophis), who daily tries to stop Ra's boat of creation, is the symbol of entropy. This concept of entropy has been referred to as "chaos" by Western Egyptologists.

Apep

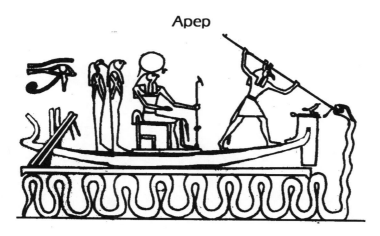

Above: Set protecting the boat of Ra from the forces of entropy (symbolized by the serpent Apep).

As expressed previously, in Neterian religion there is also no concept of a "devil" or "demon" as is conceived in the Judeo-Christian or Islamic traditions. Rather, it is understood that manifestations of detrimental situations and adversities arise as a result of unrighteous actions. These unrighteous actions are due to the "Setian" qualities in a human being. Set is the Neteru of egoism and the negative qualities which arise from egoism. Egoism is the idea of individuality based on identification with the body and mind only as being who one is. One has no deeper awareness of their deeper spiritual essence, and thus no understanding of their connectedness to all other objects (includes persons) in creation and the Divine Self. When the ego is under the control of the higher nature, it fights the forces of entropy (as above). However, when beset with ignorance, it leads to the degraded states of human existence. The vices (egoism, selfishness, extraverted ness, wonton sexuality (lust), jealousy, envy, greed, gluttony) are a result.

Set

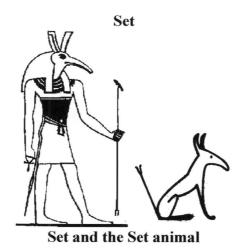

Set and the Set animal

The Great Awakening of Neterian Religion

"Nehast"

Nehast means to "wake up," to Awaken to the higher existence. In the Prt m Hru Text it is said:

Nuk pa Neter aah Neter Ziah asha ren[7]

"I am that same God, the Supreme One, who has myriad of mysterious names."

The goal of all the Neterian disciplines is to discover the meaning of "Who am I?," to unravel the mysteries of life and to fathom the depths of eternity and infinity. This is the task of all human beings and it is to be accomplished in this very lifetime.

This can be done by learning the ways of the Neteru, emulating them and finally becoming like them, Akhus, (enlightened beings), walking the earth as giants and accomplishing great deeds such as the creation of the universe!

Udjat
The Eye of Heru is a quintessential symbol of awakening to Divine Consciousness, representing the concept of Nehast.

INTRODUCTION

What is Creation?
Who Created Creation?
What is the Purpose of Creation?

These questions have been asked time and time again over the course of history. Is there any answer? The Ancient Egyptian Sages thought so and they recorded their discoveries in the form of a Mystical philosophy (*Shetaut*) called *Pauti.* This volume focuses on the Ancient Egyptian philosophy of the Pauti and how it contains important mystical teachings about the nature of Creation, God and human existence.

There are several creation myths in Ancient Egypt. There are three major myth related to the Ancient Egyptian Trinity of Amun-Ra-Ptah in which Creation emanates from Neberdjer (Nebertcher) or the Absolute, Supreme Self, in the form of a Trinity. There are also myths related to Creation as having emanated from each individual member of the Trinity (Amun, Ra, or Ptah).

There are also myths related to the gods Khepri and Asar (Osiris) and how he created the world by uttering their own name. The goddess has also been recognized as the source of Creation as well. These myths may appear to be contradictory but this understanding occurs when the deeper aspects of Ancient Egyptian Mysticism are not well understood.

Yoga is the study and practice of wisdom and spiritual disciplines which will allow a human being to discover the source of all existence and to attain the highest level of self-discovery which leads to inner peace, contentment and unobstructed joy.

Yoga is the practice of mental, physical and spiritual disciplines which lead to self-control and self-discovery by purifying the mind, body and spirit, so as to discover the deeper spiritual essence which lies within every human being and object in the universe. In essence, the goal of yoga practice is to unite or *yoke* one's individual consciousness with universal or cosmic consciousness. Therefore, Ancient Egyptian religious practice, especially in terms of the rituals and other practices of the Ancient Egyptian temple system known as *Shetaut Neter* (the way of the hidden Supreme Being), may be termed as a yoga system: *Egyptian Yoga.* In this sense, religion, in its purest form, is a yoga system, as it seeks to reunite people with their true and original source.

The disciplines of Yoga fall under five major categories. These are: *Yoga of Wisdom, Yoga of Devotional Love, Yoga of Meditation, Tantric Yoga* and *Yoga of Selfless Action.* Within these categories there are subsidiary forms which are part of the main disciplines. The emphasis in the Osirian Myth is on the Yoga of Wisdom, Yoga of Devotional Love and Yoga of Selfless Action. The important point to remember is that all aspects of yoga can and should be used in an integral fashion to effect an efficient and harmonized spiritual movement in the practitioner. Therefore, while there may be an area of special emphasis, other elements are bound to become part of the yoga program as needed. For example, while a yogin may place emphasis on the Yoga of Wisdom, they may also practice Devotional Yoga and Meditation Yoga along with the wisdom studies.

So the practice of any discipline that leads to oneness with Supreme Consciousness can be called yoga. If you study, rationalize and reflect upon the teachings, you are practicing *Yoga of Wisdom*. If you meditate upon the teachings and your Higher Self, you are practicing *Yoga of Meditation*. If you practice rituals which identify you with your spiritual nature, you are practicing *Yoga of Ritual Identification* (which is part of the Yoga of Wisdom and the Yoga of Devotional Love of the Divine). If you develop your physical nature and psychic energy centers, you are practicing *Serpent Power* (*Kundalini or Uraeus*) *Yoga* (which is part of Tantric Yoga). If you practice living according to the teachings of ethical behavior and selflessness, you are practicing *Yoga of Action* (Maat) in daily life. If you practice turning your attention towards the Divine by developing love for the Divine, then it is called *Devotional Yoga* or *Yoga of Divine Love*. The practitioner of yoga is called a yogin (male practitioner) or yogini (female practitioner), and one who has attained the culmination of yoga (union with the Divine) is called a yogi. In this manner, yoga has been developed into many disciplines which may be used in an integral fashion to achieve the same goal: Enlightenment. Therefore, the aspirant should learn about all of the paths of yoga and choose those elements which best suit his/her personality or practice them all in an integral, balanced way.

Enlightenment is the term used to describe the highest level of spiritual awakening. It means attaining such a level of spiritual awareness that one discovers the underlying unity of the entire universe as well as the fact that the source of all creation is the same source from which the innermost Self within every human heart arises.

All forms of spiritual practice are directed toward the goal of assisting every individual to discover the true essence of the universe both externally, in physical creation, and internally, within the human heart, as the very root of human consciousness. Thus, many terms are used to describe the attainment of the goal of spiritual knowledge and the eradication of spiritual ignorance. Some of these terms are: *Enlightenment, Resurrection, Salvation, The Kingdom of Heaven, Moksha or Liberation, Buddha Consciousness, One With The Tao, Self-realization, to Know Thyself,* etc.

The term religion comes from the Latin "*Relegare*" which uses the word roots "*RE*", which means "*BACK*", and "*LIGON*", which means "*to hold, to link, to bind.*" Therefore, the essence of true religion is that of linking back, specifically, linking its followers back to their original source and innermost essence. In this sense the terms "religion" and "yoga" are synonymous. This source which is the underlying reality behind every object in Creation is described as unborn, undying, eternal and immortal, and is known by an endless number of names, some of which are: Consciousness, Self, Higher Self, God, Goddess, Supreme Being, Divine Self, Eternal Self, Soul, Pure Consciousness, Brahman, All, Allah, Jehovah, Neter Neteru, Creator, Absolute, Heavenly Father, Divine Mother, Great Spirit. These various names, while arising from various traditions and separate cultures, in reality represent the same divine and transcendental principle.

So the study and understanding of Creation is an integral part of a persons yogic movement towards spiritual enlightenment. Therefore, this volume will focus on the principles of understanding mystical philosophy. It will focus on the most important creation myth since all the creation myth of Ancient Egypt are related to the most ancient one, The Creation based on the Theology of the Ancient Egyptian city of Anu. Anunian Theology is based on the understanding that there is one Supreme Divinity from which all other deities, known as Pauti, and indeed nature itself arises. Thus, let us begin our journey of discovery of *THE MYSTERIES OF SHETAUT PAUTI.*

Who Was the Founder of Neterianism and What is the Lineage of the Neterian Teaching

One of the most important questions in life for followers of any religion is who started it? The next important question is what is the lineage of the spiritual teaching, that is, how was it transmitted down through history? In order to understand who founded Neterianism, the teaching of Shetaut Neter, we must also understand the origins of creation. In the sacred scriptures of Shetaut Neter we are told that Creation is a cycle. That is, that Creation occurs cyclically. God brings creation into existence and then dissolves it again.

The Sun-god of night surrounded by the five-headed serpent of 'Many Faces'. On his head is the beetle of Khepri the the rising sun of the following day.

The current cycle of Creation began around the year 36,000 B.C.E. In the beginning there was nothing more than a watery mass, a primeval ocean, called Nun. Nun is the body of Khepri. Prior to the creation, Khepri remained in a recumbent posture. He rested on the back of the great serpent Asha-hrau ("many faces"). From that Nun the Divine Spirit arose by stimulating Asha-hrau to move and churn the ocean. Then he named himself Khepri, Creator. Khepri called

out his own name and   ⬤ ⌐◻ dchn – vibrations were infused in the ocean and waves vere formed. Just as there are many waves in the ocean with many shapes and sizes, the objects of the world came into being in the form of elements, Ra (fire), Shu (air-space), Tefnut (water), Geb (earth), Nut (ether). Everything in creation emanates from the Nun or primordial ocean, and expresses in the form of elements in succeeding levels of denseness. These elements also manifest in the form of the opposites of Creation (man-woman, up-down, white-black) which appear to be exclusive and separate from each other, but which are in reality complements to each other.

ABOVE: LORD KHEPRI, FOUNDER OF NETERIANISM

Khepri and the Creation Myth

Khepri congealed the Nun, his own body, into all the forms of Creation. The first spot that was congealed from the Nun is called Benben, the first place, the Ben-Ben dot, □, of Creation. That dot is the center point in the symbol of Khepr-Ra $. That dot is the very point at the top of the Pyramid mr-Obelisk, tekhnu. The pyramid-obelisk symbolizes the mound that formed from that initial spot. Khepri sat atop the hill of Creation and all solid ground took form underneath him.

Khepri then bought forth Creation by emerging in a boat. The Nun waters lifted him and his boat up with his great arms. He brought nine divinities with him in that boat, lesser gods and goddesses, to help him sustain the Creation and lead human beings on the righteous path to life and spiritual enlightenment.

Having created Creation, Khepri now sails the ocean, which has now become Creation itself, with his divinities, on the divine boat. Khepri-Ra and the *pauti*, Company of gods and goddesses, travels in the Boat of Millions of Years, which traverses the heavens, and thereby sustains creation through the wake of the boat that sends ripples (vibrations) throughout Creation.

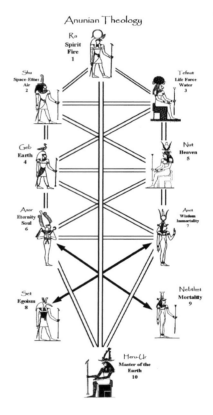

The act of "Sailing" signifies the motion in creation. Motion implies that events occur in the realm of time and space relative to each other, thus, the phenomenal universe comes into existence as a mass of moving essence we call the elements. Prior to this motion, there was the primeval state of being without any form and without existence in time or space. The gods and goddesses of the boat form the court of Kheper-Ra. As Ra, the Supreme Being governed the earth for many thousands of years. He created the world, the planets, the stars and the galaxies; he also created animals, as well as men and women. In the beginning, men and women revered the Divine, but after living for a very long time, they began to take Ra for granted. They became arrogant and vain. Ra sent his daughter, Hetheru, to punish them, but she forgot her way and became lost in the world. Then He left for his abode in heaven and gave the earthly throne to his son Shu, and daughter, Tefnut. After a long period of time, they turned over the throne to their children, Geb and Nut. After some time again, Geb and Nut gave the throne to their children, Asar and Aset, and so on in a line of succession throughout history, down to the Pharaohs of Kamit.

Lord Khepri manifests as Neberdjer, "All-encompassing Divinity." Aspirants are to say:

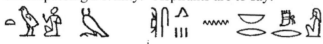

tu-a m shems n Neberdjer
"I am a follower of Neberdjer[ii]

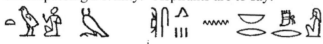

er sesh n Kheperu
in accordance with the writings of Lord Kheperu"

So, the Shetaut Neter "Mystery teachings" were originally given by the Creator, Khepri. In his capacity as Creator he is known as *Shetaut Kheperu, "hidden Creator of forms."* Lord Djehuti codified these Mystery teachings into the hieroglyphic texts. The teaching Shetaut Neter or Mysteries, given by Lord Khepri that was codified by Lord Djehuti was taken by Lord Asar who developed the *Shedy* or means to penetrate the mysteries. The disciplines of Shedy (study of philosophy, Divine Worship, Maat-right action and Meditation) were taught to Lady Hetheru and Lady Aset and other divinities by Lord Djehuti. Djehuti, Asar, Aset, Hetheru taught the Priests and Priestesses the mysteries. Those teachings of Shetaut Neter and Shedy have come down through history in varied forms, sometimes openly and at others, in secrecy through initiates who have kept the teachings alive, and in latent form through traditions kept alive in varied

spiritual traditions that have developed based on the Neterian teachings.

So Lord Khepri imparted his knowledge to the divinities, and especially to his son Djehuti . Thus, Lord Khepri, the Self Created Divinity, is the founder of Shetaut Neter. The codifier was his first main disciple, Djehuti. Djehuti has the body of a man and the head of an Ibis bird. He also has another form as a baboon. The teaching that Lord Khepri gave to Djehuti became known as *Shetitu* and it was conveyed through the *Medu Neter* (hieroglyphic texts).

"Medu Neter"

The teachings of the Neterian Traditions are conveyed in the scriptures of the Neterian Traditions.

Above: Lord Djehuti imparted the teaching he learned from Khepri to goddess Hetheru (here in the form of a cow goddess). She became lost in the world and forgot her true identity. He showed her how to discover her true Self, how to know herself and how to find her way back to heaven, to her father Ra. Here Djehuti is shown presenting to Hetheru, the healed right eye of Ra, her true essence.

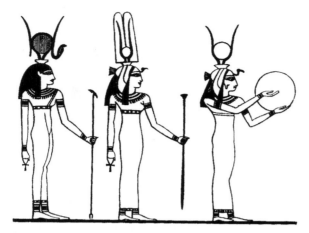

Above: Hetheru as Queen

Lord Khep-Ra knew that human beings needed guidance, so he sent his great grandchildren, Asar and Aset, to be teachers and role models for human beings on earth. Lord Djehuti also imparted the hidden knowledge of life to Aset and Asar, so that they would lead people on earth in a righteous manner, showing them the path of peace, prosperity and spiritual enlightenment. Asar and Aset established the Shetaut Neter, "Divine Mysteries," ritual worship and Ancient Egyptian religion. When human beings become too involved in the world they forget their true nature, and so the Temple,

Het Neter {House of the Divinity {God(dess)}-Temple}, was created, where the pressure of the world can be relieved, and an association with something other than the worldly perspective (i.e., with Divinity) can occur.

Temple of Aset, Egypt, Africa

Such a place and its teaching are needed so that the mind can become aware of higher possibilities and turn away from *umt-ab*- "mental dullness" due to *Khemn*, "ignorance," and be led to *Nehast* –"Resurrection, spiritual awakening," *Akhu*, "enlightenment" and so that human beings may become *Sheps*- "nobility, honor, venerable-ness, honored ancestors."

Above: *Aset nurses baby Heru*

So, Aset learned the Mystery teachings from Lord Djehuti. Aset is the ancient African prototype of the mother and child which is popular all over Africa, and also in Christian and Indian iconography with the birth of Jesus and Krishna, respectively. The mother is the first teacher. Aset not only raised Heru, but also initiated him into the mysteries of life and creation, with the teaching she learned from Djehuti and Khepri, in order to enlighten him and make him strong for the battle of life. Heru became a powerful initiate and became the model for all human beings who strive to master the lower forces of nature and to discover their higher essential nature.

Heru is the redeemer, the challenger, the one who stands up for his father, Asar, and liberates him from the imprisonment of death. Heru represents spiritual aspiration and success in the spiritual path. Heru reestablishes order after defeating the evil Set, and takes the throne of Kamit. In his form as Heru Behdet, Heru is a warrior. He fights for truth, justice and freedom for all.

Heru, the redeemer, the warrior, the greatest advocate of Asar (the soul) and triumphant aspirant is the one who leads the aspirant to the initiation hall. As seen above, Heru is often the one shown leading the aspirant by the hand, into the inner shrine. In rituals, the priest wears a Heru mask in the context of a ritual theatrical ceremony of the temple that is meant to awaken the glory of the Neterian teaching.

Lord Khepri

The Deities and Myth of The Creation

The characters or deities of the Creation can be seen as spiritual principles which a person who considers him or her self to be a spiritual aspirant should follow. If these principles are followed they allow the practitioner to develop those spiritual qualities and these lead to spiritual enlightenment. They can be seen as a ladder for climbing from the bottom of Creation (the earth) to the top or Creation (Heru-Divine Self). In order to understand their relationships and spiritual message it will be necessary to review the Ausarian Resurrection Myth. Therefore, a summary of the myth and its mystical teaching is included below.

The Myth of Ra, Asar, Aset and Heru

Lord Ra

The Creation

In the beginning there was no Creation, no sky, no earth, no people and no planets or sun. There was only a primeval ocean without form. Then, out of this ocean emerged Ra. Ra was lifted out of the ocean by Nun, the ocean itself. With him he brought into existence the nine gods and goddesses of Creation. two of these gods and goddesses were Asar and Aset. They came to earth in order to lead human beings to discover the proper way to live and to attain happiness and spiritual enlightenment.

The Story of Asar, Aset and Heru

Asar and Aset dedicated themselves to the welfare of humanity and sought to spread civilization throughout the earth, even as far as India and China. Sometimes Asar would travel around the world without Aset at his side. At other times they would travel together.

Aset continued to rule over Egypt while Asar was traveling around the world. During the absence of Asar from his kingdom, his brother Set had no opportunity to make innovations in the state, because Aset was extremely vigilant in governing the country, and always upon her guard and watchful for any irregularity or unrighteousness.

Upon Asar' return from touring the world and carrying the teachings of wisdom abroad, there was merriment and rejoicing throughout the land. However, one day after Asar' return, through his lack of vigilance, became intoxicated and slept with Set's wife, Nebthet. Nebthet loves Asar and seized the opportunity to sleep with Asar at a time when he was not vigilant since she looks just like Aset, except for her headdress. Nebthet, as a result of the union with Asar, begot Anubis.

Set, who represents the personification of evil forces, plotted in jealousy and anger (the blinding passion that prevents forgiveness and understanding) to usurp the throne and conspired to kill Asar. Set secretly got the measurements of Asar and constructed a coffin. Through trickery, Set was able to get Asar to "try on" the coffin for size. While Asar was resting in the coffin, Set and his assistants locked it and then dumped it into the Nile river.

The coffin made its way to the coast of Syria where it became embedded in the earth and from it grew a tree with the most pleasant aroma in the form of a Djed or Djed. The Djed is the symbol of Asar's back. It has four horizontal lines in relation to a firmly established, straight column. The Djed column is symbolic of the upper energy centers (chakras) that relate to the levels of consciousness of the spirit.

The King of Syria was out walking and as he passed by the tree, he immediately fell in love with the pleasant aroma, so he had the tree cut down and brought to his palace. Aset (Auset, Ast), Asar' wife, who is the personification of the life giving, mother force in creation and in all humans, went to Syria in search of Asar. Her search led her to the palace of the Syrian King where she took a job as the nurse of the King's son. Every evening, Aset would put the boy into the "fire" to consume his mortal parts, thereby transforming him to immortality. Fire is symbolic of both physical and mental purification. Most importantly, fire implies wisdom, the light of truth, illumination and energy which burns away ignorance and egoism. Aset, by virtue of her qualities, has the power to bestow immortality through the transformative power of her symbolic essence. She symbolizes intuitional wisdom which leads to the eradication of mortal consciousness and the birth of immortal continuousness. Aset then told the king that Asar, her husband, was inside the pillar he made from the tree. He graciously gave her the pillar (Djed) and she returned with it to Kamit (Kmt, Egypt). With the assistance of the crocodile god Sebek, Aset brought the body of Asar back to Kemet.

Upon her return to Kmt, Aset went to the papyrus swamps where she lay over Asar's dead body and fanned him with her wings, infusing him with new life. In this manner Aset revived Asar through her power of love and wisdom, and then they united once more. From their union was conceived a son, Heru (Horus), with the assistance of the gods Djehuti and Amon. Heru, therefore, was born from the union of the spirit of Asar and the life giving power of Aset (physical nature). Thus, Heru represents the union of spirit and matter, and the renewed life of Asar, his rebirth.

One evening, as Set was hunting in the papyrus swamps, he came upon Aset and Asar. In a rage of passion he dismembered the body of Asar into several pieces and scattered the pieces throughout the land. In this way, it is Set, the brute force of our bodily impulses and lower desires that "dismembers" our higher intellect. Instead of oneness and unity, we see multiplicity and separateness which give rise to egoistic (selfish) and violent behavior. The Great Mother, Aset, once again set out to search, now for the pieces of Asar, with the help of Anubis and Nebthet.

After searching all over the world, they found all the pieces of Asar's body, except for his phallus which was eaten by a fish. In Eastern Hindu-Tantra mythology, the God Shiva, who is the equivalent of Asar, also lost his phallus in one story. In Ancient Egyptian and Hindu-Tantra mythology, this loss represents seminal retention and celibacy in order to channel the sexual energy to the higher spiritual centers, thereby transforming it into spiritual energy. Aset, through her love, devotion and wisdom, and with the help of Apuat and Nebthet re-membered the pieces of Asar, all except the phallus which was eaten by a fish. Asar thus regained life and became king of the realm of the dead.

Aset took Heru into hiding so that he could grow up safely away from Set. One day Set sent an evil scorpion to find Heru and kill him so that he could not grow up to challenge him for the throne of Kemet. The scorpion found Heru and stung and killed him. When Aset found out about this she was so grief stricken that her cry was heard to the farthest reaches of the universe. When Ra, the Supreme Being, heard it, he stopped his movement. This effectively brought the entire universe to a standstill. In response to Aset, Ra sent Djehuti to assist Aset. Djehuti carried special words of power which allowed him to revive Heru.

When Heru became a young man, Asar returned from the realm of the dead and encouraged him to take up arms (vitality, wisdom, courage, strength of will) and establish truth, justice and righteousness in the world by challenging Set, its current ruler.

The scorpion goddess Selket assisted Aset in her time of sorrow over the death of Heru and Asar. She comforted Aset in her time of grief. She acted as the voice of reason, suggesting that Aset should call out to the Boat of Ra for assistance when Heru was killed. This episode attests to the understanding that even though Selket is a scorpion, like the one which killed Heru, her power to cause injury was turned to a positive end. So the same mental energy, as symbolized by the scorpion, can be used to promote negativity by associating with the ego (Set) or positive spiritual movement when aligned with wisdom (Aset).

Above: The Boat of Ra

The Battle of Heru (Heru) and Set

The battle between Heru and Set took many twists, sometimes one seeming to get the upper hand and sometimes the other, yet neither one gaining a clear advantage in order to decisively win. At one point, Aset tried to help Heru by catching Set, but due to the pity and compassion she felt towards him, she set him free. In a passionate rage, Heru cut off her head and went off by himself in a frustrated state. Even Heru is susceptible to passion which leads to performing deeds that one later regrets. Set found Heru and gouged out Heru's eyes. During this time, Heru was overpowered by the evil of Set. He became blinded to truth (as signified by the loss of his eyes) and thus, was unable to do battle (act with Maat) with Set. His power of sight was later restored by Hethor and Djehuti. Hethor is the Goddess of passionate love, desire and fierce power, who also represents the left Eye of Ra. She is the fire spitting, destructive power of light, which dispels the darkness (blindness) of ignorance. Djehuti represents knowledge and right reasoning, the power of the mind to see spiritual truth. He brings subtlety of intellect to understand the deeper meaning of the teachings.

When the conflict resumed, the two contendants went before the court of the Psedjet divinities (company of the nine gods who ruled over creation, headed by Ra). Set, promising to end the fight and restore Heru to the throne, invited Heru to spend the night at his house, but Heru soon found out that Set had evil intentions when he tried to have intercourse with him. The uncontrolled Set also symbolizes unrestricted sexual activity. Therefore, all sexual desires should be pursued in accordance with moral and intellectual principles which dictate rules of propriety that lead to health, and personal, societal and spiritual order (Maat). Juxtaposed against this aspect of Set (uncontrolled sexual potency and desire) is Heru in the form of ithyphallic (erect phallus) Min, who represents not only the control of sexual desire, but its sublimation as well (see Min and Hethor). Min symbolizes the power which comes from the sublimation of the sexual energy.

On the next page: The Goddess Hetheru, the right Eye of Ra.

Through more treachery and deceit, Set attempted to destroy Heru with the help of the Psedjet, by tricking them into believing that Heru was not worthy of the throne. Asar sent a letter pleading with the Psedjet to do what is correct. Heru, as the son of Asar, should be the rightful heir to the throne. All but two of them (the Psedjet) agreed because Heru, they said, was too young to rule. Asar then sent them a second letter (scroll of papyrus with a message) reminding them that even they cannot escape judgment for their deeds; they will be judged in the end when they have to finally go to the West (abode of the dead).

This signifies that even the gods and goddesses cannot escape judgment for their deeds and that their existence is finite. Since all that exists is only a manifestation of the absolute reality which goes beyond time and space, that which is in the realm of time and space (humans, spirits, gods, angels, neteru) are all bound by its laws.

Following the receipt of Asar's scroll (letter), Heru was crowned King of Egypt. Set accepted the decision and made peace with Heru. All the gods and goddesses rejoiced. Thus ends the legend of Asar, Aset, and Heru.

Above: the eyes of Ra (Also the eyes of Heru- the sun and moon)

A SUMMARY OF THE MYSTICAL SYMBOLISM OF THE STORY OF ASAR ASET AND HERU

Asar represents the human soul which has incarnated on earth in human form. Thus, he represents the innermost reality of all human beings. The soul falls in love with life and the physical human existence which is symbolized by Nebthet. Nebthet represents physical pleasure. When the soul forgets its true nature, it becomes overpowered by the lower nature, the ego, as symbolized by Set.

Therefore, Asar's brother, Set, symbolizes egoism and all of the negative qualities which a human being can develop when they are ignorant of their higher essence. The story symbolically relates how the unbridled negative emotions and desires of a human being (the ego), essentially hacks to pieces the soul and attempts to stop any chance for it to reincarnate in order to seek redemption and enlightenment. Set also represents the treachery of the world, that which seems to be a promise of pleasure, but is in reality a snare which enslaves the soul to the myriad forms of misery of human existence. Set represents the distractions and pressure of life to indulge in the pleasures of the senses. Thus, Heru represents spiritual aspiration, the desire to study and practice the teachings and the inner spiritual strength which is required to sublimate the ego and to succeed in the struggle of life.

Aset is the wisdom which allows a person to put together the understanding of their higher reality, the Spirit. She is also the knowledge of how to call to the Divine in order to discover one's spiritual essence. She, together with the inner spirit, as symbolized by the spirit of Asar, is also the power within the heart which gives a person encouragement and strength to face the adversities of the world and then to call out to the Divine in order to attain enlightenment. So when a desire to learn spirituality emerges, it is the spirit of Asar which is urging the aspirant onward. Then that movement towards spirituality is nurtured by the goddess as a mother who brings forth new life and nourishes it to health and growth by protecting it from the elements and from all negative influences until it is strong enough to stand on its own. Apuat represents the development of intellectual discrimination, the ability to understand truth from untruth, reality from unreality, and Sebek represents the power of the lower nature, the physical body, when it is sublimated and placed in the service of the Higher Self.

For a more detailed study of the Ausarian Resurrection Myth it is highly recommended that you review the books, "The Ausarian Resurrection: The Ancient Egyptian Bible" and "The Mystical Teachings of the Ausarian Resurrection: Initiation Into The Third Level of Shetaut Asar" by Dr. Muata Ashby.

The Pauti: Nine Principles of Creation According to The Theology of Anu
(Selected verses from The Ausarian Resurrection Myth of Ancient Egypt)

5   In the beginning, there was the primeval ocean, Nu, and from it arose Ra, who was lifted up from the depths of the ocean by Nu. Upon his emergence this magnificent God created all that came into being from his own self and he existed within his creation as one exists within one's own body. He emanated Shu and Tefnut and they in turn gave rise to Nut and Geb. The goddess Nut and the god Geb were united in amorous embrace since they had loved each other so deeply from the beginning of time. Their embrace was so close that no other living being could exist in the world.

6   From their union Nut became pregnant, but Ra had decreed that they should be separated and that Nut could not give birth in any month of the year. At this time he also decided to retreat as an active participant in his creation and to abide in heaven wherein all who would seek him must go. From this position he supports creation as he traverses in the form of the sun making it possible for life to exist and flourish. In the morning he is known as Kheper, at noon he is known as Ra and at sunset he is known as Tem.

7   Also from here he witnesses all of the activities and events of creation. In his absence he created Djehuti, his minister and messenger through whom he, Ra, would manage and sustain his creation.

8   Ra instituted himself as the sustainer of creation during the day and illumines creation as the sun, ☉, while setting Djehuti up in the form of the baboon to watch over creation at night as the moon, ☽.

The Birth of Osiris and Isis

9   Having become pregnant as a result of her sexual union with Geb, Nut gave birth to Osiris, Set, Isis, Nephthys, Hathor, Maat, and Djehuti.

10   Djehuti, who being wise and caring for Nut, was able to win the seventieth part of each day of the year and to have these added up and added to the year. These Epagomenal Days or "the five days over the year" he added to the three hundred and sixty days of which the year formerly consisted. These five days are to this day called the "Epagomenae," that is, the "superadded", and they are observed as the birthdays of the gods. On the first of these days, Osiris was born, and as he came into the world a voice was heard saying, *"The Lord of All, Nebertcher, is born."*

10   Upon the second of these days was born Horus the Elder. Upon the third day Set was born, who came into the world neither at the proper time nor by the right way, but he forced a passage through a wound which he made in his mother's side. Upon the fourth day Isis was born in the marshes of Egypt, and upon the fifth day Nephthys was born. As regards the fathers of these children, the first two are said to have been begotten by Ra, Isis by Djehuti, and Set and Nephthys by Geb. Therefore, since the third of the superadded days was the birthday of Set, the kings considered it to be unlucky and in consequence, they neither transacted any business in it, nor even suffered themselves to take any refreshment until the evening.

11   They further add that Set married Nephthys and that Isis and Osiris, having a mutual affection, enjoyed each other in their mother's womb even before they were born, and that from this union sprang Horus the Elder (whom the Greeks Apollo). Osiris and Isis gave birth to Horus, and Osiris and Nephthys gave birth to Anubis.

UNDERSTANDING THE PROCESS OF CREATION

The Mysteries of Anu are considered to be the oldest exposition of the teachings of Creation and they formed a foundation for the unfoldment of the teachings of mystical spirituality which followed in the mysteries of the city of *Hetkaptah* through the Divinity in the name Ptah, and the Mysteries of *Newt (Waset or Thebes)*, through the Divinity in the name Amun. With each succeeding exposition, the teaching becomes more and more refined until it reaches its quintessence in the *Hymns of Amun*. Thus, while each of the divinities in the Ancient Egyptian Trinity (Amun-Ra-Ptah) are related, in their own tutelary way they assume the form of the *High Divinity* or *Supreme Being* with name and form. However, as we have seen, they are only representations or symbols (representation with name and form) of the transcendental androgynous Divinity which is without name or form who is referred to as Nebertcher. This understanding holds vast implications for the comprehension of Ancient Egyptian Religion and its message in reference to the human soul because the human soul is related to Nebertcher just as the Trinity is related to Nebertcher.

The process of creation is explained in the form of a cosmological system for better understanding. Cosmology is a branch of philosophy dealing with the origin, processes, and structure of the universe. Cosmogony is the astrophysical study of the creation and evolution of the universe. Both of these disciplines are inherent facets of Egyptian philosophy through the main religious systems or Companies of the gods and goddesses. A company of gods and goddesses is a group of deities which symbolize a particular cosmic force or principle which emanates from the all-encompassing Supreme Being, from which they have emerged. The Self or Supreme Being manifests creation through the properties and principles represented by the *Pauti* (Company of gods and goddesses-cosmic laws of nature). The system or company of gods and goddesses of Anu is regarded as the oldest, and forms the basis of the Osirian Trinity. It is expressed in the diagram below.

Nun
⇩
Ra-Tem
⇩
Hetheru-Djehuti-Maat
⇩
Shu ⇔ Tefnut
⇩
Geb⇔Nut
⇖   ⇩   ⇘

Set — Nebthet   Asar ⇔ Aset   Asar⇔ Nebthet
                        ⇩   ⇩
                      Heru-Ur   Apuat

The diagram above shows that *Pauti*, or the creative principles which are embodied in the primordial gods and goddesses of creation, emanated from the Supreme Being. Ra or Ra-Tem arose out of the *"Nu"*, the Primeval waters, the hidden essence, and began sailing the *"Boat of Millions of Years"* which included the company of gods and goddesses. On his boat emerged the "Neteru" or cosmic principles of creation. The neteru of the Pauti are Ra-Atum (Tem, Tum, Atum), Shu, Tefnut, Geb, Nut, Asar, Aset, Set, and Nebthet. Hethor, Djehuti and Maat represent attributes of the Supreme Being as the very *stuff* or *substratum* which makes up creation. Shu, Tefnut, Geb, Nut, Asar (Osiris), Aset (Isis), Set, and Nebthet (Nephthys) represent the principles upon which creation manifests. Apuat or Anubis is not part of the Ennead. He represents the feature of intellectual discrimination in the Osirian myth. "Sailing" signifies the beginning of motion in creation. Motion implies that events occur in the realm of time and space, thus, the phenomenal universe comes into existence as a mass of moving essence we call the elements. Prior to this motion, there was the primeval state of being without any form and without existence in time or space.

Picture 1: Tem in the Solar Boat wearing the double crown, sitting within the sundisk.

The "High God" and The Gods and Goddesses

There were several "High God" systems in Ancient Egyptian Mythology. High God means that the highest God or Goddess within that particular system of theology is considered to be the original deity from which all others emanated as cosmic forces. Thus, Osiris is known as *Pa Neter* or *The God* (High God) and Creation is composed of the cosmic forces which originated from Osiris. The cosmic forces are known as *neters* or gods and goddesses. It is important to understand that the High Gods and Goddesses as well as the Egyptian Trinities originated from the same transcendental Supreme Being which was without name or form, but was referred to as *Neter Neteru* (Neter of Neters - Supreme Being above all gods and goddesses) and *Neb-er-tcher*. There were several forms of the Trinity in Ancient Egyptian religion depending on the geographic locality where the teaching was espoused. These included: Amun-Mut-Khons, Ptah-Sekhmet-Nefertem, Horus-Hathor-Harsomtus (Horus the Younger), Khnum-Anukis-Satis, Ptah-Seker-Ausar (Osiris). However, the most popular Trinity throughout all of Ancient Egypt was that of Osiris-Isis-Horus.

In this manner, the initiate is to understand that all of the gods and goddesses are in reality symbols, with names and forms, which represent the Divine in the varied manifest forms of nature. This produces a two aspected format of religion in which there is a *personal* aspect and a *transpersonal* aspect of God. The personal aspect is fixed in time and space with a name and form. This form is readily understood by the masses of human beings with ordinary spiritual awareness and is used in myths and stories. The second aspect, the *transpersonal* side, points our interest towards that which lies beyond the symbolic form. This is the *unmanifest* form of the Divine as it is expressed in the mystical teachings of religious mythology. Thus, the High God is a personal symbol or representation, with a name and form, of the nameless, formless, unmanifest and transcendental Supreme Being.

Single Supreme, Transcendental Being
Pa Neter - Neter Neteru - Nebertcher
(unmanifest realm beyond time and space - names and forms)
↓
High Gods and Goddesses manifesting as a Trinity: *Amun-Ra-Ptah; Osiris-Isis-Horus*

The Transcendental, Absolute Spirit gives rise to the High Gods and Goddesses. All of the gods and goddesses in the Ennead have emanated from this most hidden and transcendental realm. This realm is the source of all that has been and will ever be and it is the sustaining force which supports and maintains creation at every moment. When the Supreme Divinity decides to end the present cycle of creation, the entire cosmos recedes back into this most hidden realm. This "end" to a cycle of creation is often termed a "flood" or "period of dissolution." Thus, all beings, as emanations from the Supreme Deity, are destined to return to the source of all creation in much the same way as a dream recedes back into consciousness when a person wakes up. In this sense, the Primeval Ocean of consciousness is like the mental substance of an individual human being. Just as the world created in a dream is absorbed back into consciousness and no longer reflects in the mind, upon waking up, so too the cosmos is "absorbed" into the Supreme Being. Thus, there is a supreme, all powerful being from which not even a single atom escapes. However, this realm can only be discovered through purity of heart. Upon making this discovery it is said that the "world has come to an end." This is because those who have discovered the truth, the absolute reality which transcends the planes of existence, now understand creation as a dream or mental projection of God. Having acquired this wisdom means that that person has attuned their consciousness to God's consciousness, and has discovered that they are and always were one with that Divinity. Now there is no more egoism. There is only consciousness of the universe as being an emanation of the one Supreme Divinity who is in the heart of all.

The Substratum of Creation

Maat, Hathor and Djehuti were not part of the Ennead, yet they played important roles in the Osirian myth. As stated earlier, the neters of the Ennead are Ra-Atum, Shu, Tefnut, Geb, Nut, Osiris, Isis, Set (Seth) and Nephthys. As stated earlier, Hathor, Djehuti and Maat represent attributes of the Supreme Being as the very *stuff* or *substratum* which makes up creation. This means that they are the elements which the creative principle uses in the act of creation. This idea may be better understood through the following simile. Consider a lump of clay. The clay can be given several forms but the substratum of any form which the clay is given, be it a pot, plate, bowl, cup, etc., will always remain the same, clay. The composition of the clay does not change. In the same manner Hathor, Maat and Djehuti represent attributes of the Supreme Being which do not change regardless of the forms which objects in creation take. Therefore, they are the constant, absolute principles among all that is changing, chaotic, transient, and therefore illusory, in human experience as well as in creation. Hathor represents the force of spiritual energy which drives the entire universe. The relentless order and synchronicity of the planets and stars, as well as the order of events which occur in the life of every human being, is symbolized by Maat, and the light of consciousness which is the underlying characteristic of all sentient life is symbolized by Djehuti.

Uatchit and Nekhebet represent the dual aspect of creation, the "Two Lands" (Upper Egypt, symbolized by the Lotus plant and Lower Egypt, symbolized by the Papyrus plant). In a mystical sense they symbolize heaven and earth, spirit and matter. However, they also represent the subtle spiritual energy known as the Arat (Serpent Power), more commonly known by the name Kundalini. The Serpent Power is the Life Force energy which sustains life and promotes the desire for action in the human being. It operates through the subtle spiritual energy centers and is symbolized by the shaft which is intertwined by serpents in the staffs of Uatchit and Nekhebet, as well as the staff of Djehuti. The unity of these two principles, which are opposite poles of the same energy, is synonymous with Enlightenment and the absolute truth.

Hetheru (Hathor) represents the Life Force energy of Ra. She is the power of Creation itself, as Creation, the manifestation of the Divine Spirit, is seen as female, and the Soul of Creation, as male. Djehuti represents the mind of God. He represents the higher intellectual capacity of the mind when it is attuned to the Divine. Djehuti the messenger of God. Maat (Ma, Maa, Mayt) represents the very order which constitutes creation. Therefore, it is said that Ra created the universe by putting Maat in the place of chaos. Maat is also represents the harmony of Creation as it expresses in the form of opposites. So she is referred to as *Maati,* the double goddess. An additional manifestation of Maati is found in the forms of Aset and Nebthet. Therefore, Creation itself is Maat. She is the mother of the universe. As such, the word *ma* has appeared in many languages from around the world in relation to the world mother. In Ancient Egypt Ma or Mut signifies mother. In India, *mata;* in English speaking countries it is *mother* or *mama;* in Spanish it is *mama,* or *madre.* Thus the principle of the universal mother has found its way into human language.

Creation without order is chaos. Consider what would happen if the elements (water, air, fire, earth) did not exist according to their set parameters. What would happen if water became flammable or if earth became gaseous? What would happen if the laws of gravity acted in reverse? There would be no consistency or order in the phenomenal universe and no way for life to exist. So Maat is the basis upon which Creation exists, and Creation is the mode in which the divine Supreme Being expresses Him/Her Self. Therefore, anything which impedes order, regularity and harmony is against Maat, Creation and God. Spiritual movement and spiritual practice are difficult in an atmosphere of unrest, agitation, disorder and turmoil. Likewise, anything which promotes order, peace, harmony, truth, justice, righteousness, etc., automatically promotes spirituality, divine awareness, spiritual wisdom and self-discovery.

In a relief above which was made for *Ptolemy IV* at Edfu, there is a depiction of the Barque of Creation which shows the King standing before the barque, with upraised arms, offering Maat to The God. At the Front of the boat is Heru-p-khart, Horus the Child, with a flail. Within the boat are Heru-merti (Horus of the two eyes implying the all encompassing divinity), Maat, Apuat, Shu, Hathor, Djehuti, and Net. Behind the King, outside of the boat, stand the gods of the senses of *Hu* (Taste) and *Saa* (Touch, feeling and understanding). At the other end, also outside of the boat, stand the gods of the senses of *Maa* (Sight) and *Setem* (Hearing). Hu and Saa were known to serve as bearers of the Eye of Horus. They were also considered to be the tongue and heart of Osiris-Ptah. Thus, they represent the vehicles through which human beings can understand and espouse the teachings of moral and spiritual wisdom.

The positioning of the gods and goddesses is of paramount importance, because it points to the understanding that the neters within the boat itself are emanations of the Divine, while those outside of the boat are effects or reflections of the creative principles. Therefore, the occupants of the boat may be understood as *absolute attributes* of the Divine, while the characters outside of the boat may be understood as *relative manifestations* of the Divine in time and space. Just as sound, light and fragrances are emanations of the objects which project them, the senses are also emanations from the consciousness of the life forms which use them. The senses therefore, are relative, dependent on the particular animal and the level of sensitivity. They have no independent existence outside of the living being(s) who/which possess them. The information brought by them is processed with the use of the mind and intellect. Therefore, they are depicted as being outside of the boat. Furthermore, even the mind and intellect are relative. Spiritual sensitivity and wisdom varies from person to person. Thus, only the Spirit is absolute. The Spirit remains the same while the physical body, personality, intellectual capacity and level of sensitivity (of the senses) are relative, transient and variable. The mind, intellect, senses and ego-personality of a human being are all transient projections of the Spirit.

So from a mystical standpoint the picture symbolizes the human ego, in the form of the King and his senses, in the act of devotional meditation on the Divine, offering Maat, 𓏤, to The God, 𓊹, (Neter), in the form of Horus, The Child. Thus, living according to the principles of Maat and turning the senses and one's personal interest toward serving the Divine allow for one's spiritual movement to unfold. Saa is closely related to Djehuti, representing intelligence or higher intellect in the human being which gets close to the cosmic mind (Djehuti) through devotion to God. Maa (sight) is closely related to Maat as the clarity of vision which allows one to live by order, justice and righteousness, and not to fall under the pressure of egoistic desires and negative thoughts.

In addition to the senses, there are two more important abstract qualities through which the Divine expresses. These are Sekhem and Heh. Sekhem is energy or power though which the universe manifests. Heh, along with his counterpart Hehet, represent eternity. They are aspects of the primeval ocean, Nu. Thus, from the eternal emanates the temporal. The universe is itself composed of a divine, eternal essence which exists according to the law and order (Maat) of the Divine (Supreme Being). The qualities of humanity (egoism, mind and senses) arise from the Divine basis or substratum. They are expressions of the Divine, which when internalized, allow for self-discovery and the awareness of eternity when externalized, they promote time and space (temporal - egoistic) awareness.

NU: THE PRIMEVAL OCEAN

Egyptian Mythology is filled with stories of gods and goddesses, but all of them are related in a harmonious manner which, when understood correctly, helps to unlock the mysteries of the human heart. Egyptian mythology begins with the existence of the Nu, the Primeval Ocean. The creation stories of the Bible, the Cabalah (Jewish Mysticism) and the Upanishads (Indian Mysticism) are remarkably similar in the notion of the original primeval formlessness and in the subsequent names and forms (differentiation and objectification of matter) which arose later.

Ancient Egyptian Shabaka Inscription:

"Ptah conceived in His heart (reasoning consciousness) all that would exist and at His utterance (the word - will, power to make manifest), created Nun, the primeval waters (unformed matter-energy).
Then, not having a place to sit Ptah causes Nun to emerge from the primeval waters as the Primeval Hill so that he may have a place to sit. Atom (Atum) then emerges and sits upon Ptah. Then came out of the waters four pairs of gods, the Ogdoad (eight gods):

From Genesis 1 (Bible):

1. In the beginning God created the heaven and the earth.
2. And the earth was without form, and void; and darkness [was] upon the face of the deep. And the Spirit of God moved upon the face of the waters.

From the Sepher (Sefir) Yezirah*:

These are the ten spheres of existence, which came out of nothing. From the spirit of the Living God emanated air, from the air, water, from the water, fire or ether, from the ether, the height and the depth, the East and the West, the North and the South.

From the Zohar:

Before God manifested Himself, when all things were still hidden in him... He began by forming an imperceptible point; this was His own thought. With this thought, He then began to construct a mysterious and holy form...the Universe.

*(Cabalism)

From the Laws of Manu (Indian):

Manu is a Sage-Creator, God of Indian Hindu-Vedic tradition who recounts the process of Creation wherein the *Self-Existent Spirit* (God) felt desire. Wishing to create all things from His own body, God created the primeval waters (Nara) and threw a seed into it. From the seed came the golden cosmic egg. The Self-Existent Spirit (Narayana) developed into Brahma (Purusha) and after a year of meditation, divided into two parts (Male and Female).

When you think of your body you don't differentiate between the left leg and the right, the lips and the face, or the fingers and the arm. In a mysterious way, you consider all the parts as a whole and call this "me." In the same way, in the state of Enlightenment, the entire universe is understood as "me." Consciousness is essentially pure until the association with the ego develops. Then multiplicity and duality appear to exist, but as the following passages explain, the multiplicity of creation is merely the forms which energy takes on as it moves and interacts in different polarities or the pairs of opposites. This concept of vibrations being the underlying cause of the phenomenal world existed within the Egyptian mystical text called *The Kybalion.* The teachings of the Kybalion will be discussed in the commentary to verse 45 of the Hymns of Amun.

From the Cabalah:

Polarity is the principle that runs through the whole of creation, and is in fact, the basis of manifestation. Polarity really means the flowing of force from a sphere of high pressure to a sphere of low pressure, high and low being always relative terms. Every sphere of energy needs to receive the stimulus of an influx of energy at higher pressure, and to have an output into a sphere of lower pressure. The source of all energy is the Great Un-manifest (God), and it makes its own way down the levels, changing its form from one to the other, till it is finally "earthed" in matter.

The pure impulse of dynamic creation is formless; and being formless, the creation it gives rise to can assume any and every form.

The following passage comes from *Lao-Tzu*, the classical Taoist writer who popularized Taoism in China at the same time that *Buddha* and *Mahavira* developed Buddhism and Jainism in India. He further illustrates the idea of undifferentiated versus differentiated consciousness.

There was something undifferentiated and yet complete, which existed before heaven and earth. Soundless and formless, it depends on nothing and does not change.
It operates everywhere and is free from danger.
It may be considered the mother of the universe.

The same idea of *"formlessness"* or *"undifferentiated"* matter occurs in the *Rig* (Rik) *Veda*, the Upanishads and the Bhagavad Gita from India as well. The only difference between the following texts is that the Gita takes all of the attributes of the manifest and un-manifest nature of divinity and incorporates them in the anthropomorphic personality of Krishna.

From the Rig Veda:

There was neither non-existence nor existence then; there was neither the realm of space nor the sky beyond. There was no distinguishing sign of night nor of day... Desire came upon that one in the beginning; that was the first seed of mind.

From the Upanishads:

There are, assuredly, two forms of the Eternal: the formed and the formless, the mortal and the immortal, the stationary and the moving, the actual and the illusory.
Gita: Chapter 9:17

I am the Father of the universe; I am the Mother, the sustainer, as well as the Grandfather. I am the goal of Vedic knowledge, I am the sacred Om, I am verily the Vedas in the form of Rik, Yaju and Sama.

More On The Ancient Egyptian Primordial Ocean

Before there was any god or goddess, even Ra or Osiris and Isis, and before there was any physical matter, the planets, the sun, animals, human beings, etc., there was the primeval ocean and from it emanated all that exists. There are stories of a primeval ocean in other cultures. Hinduism also includes teachings in reference to the primeval ocean and the Christian Bible begins with creation emanating out of primeval waters, in the book of Genesis. The oldest notion and greatest emphasis on the concept of the primeval ocean comes from Ancient Egypt.

In the same manner that waves arise out of the ocean, and appear to be of different shapes, sizes and textures, the objects of the phenomenal universe, the sun, stars, planets trees, animals and all living beings, arise out of this primeval ocean. But this rising did not only occur once in the "beginning of time;" it is continually occurring. All objects in nature are continuously sustained by an "unseen" force which modern science cannot fully explain. However, science does explain some characteristics of the phenomenal universe and these reveal an ocean of energy wherein all things are interrelated and bound together, as opposed to the ordinary thinking of a universe full of separate objects which are composed of different elements. In fact, modern science reveals that all objects in the universe are composed of the same "stuff." All of the "elements" have the same basis, energy. Further, all matter is merely a manifestation of that same essence, but in different modes of manifestation. This facet of matter was explained thousands of years ago by the Sages of mystical wisdom.

The Sages have shown that consciousness or pure awareness is the basis of all matter, just as when you are not thinking, there are no thoughts or vibrations in the consciousness of your mind. In the same way, this universe is a manifestation of the thought process of the Supreme Being. Therefore, it is possible to have an infinite number of elements and combinations of those elements just as it is possible for you to create anything in your mind out of your consciousness when applied towards the imaginative and dream processes.

When the body dies, it returns to the earth from whence it arose. Where does the soul go? It returns to the ocean of consciousness, as represented by the Duat, and if it is not enlightened, returns to this Physical Plane of existence to have more human experiences. When enlightenment is attained through the practice of yoga, one communes with the ocean of pure and infinite consciousness which is an ever existing reality beyond the grasp of those who are devoid of spiritual sensitivity. Your limited mind is like a wave in the ocean of the Supreme Being. However, though the waves seem to be separate and you seem to be alone, in reality God is always there and is the very fabric of all physical objects as well as the very source and sustenance of human consciousness. It is due to the distractions of the mind caused by desires, illusions, cravings, longings and ignorance that the innermost recesses of your unconscious mind is veiled from conscious awareness. Nevertheless, the exterior world and the internal world are nothing but manifestations of the primeval waters, God, the Higher Self within all beings.

When you delve deeply into the mysteries of the ocean of consciousness within your mind, you are able to discover the deeper truths about your real essence, origin and purpose. This is the process called *Sheti*. When the wisdom teachings are studied deeply and the mystical implications are understood, a special form of transformation occurs which leads to the discovery of the highest spiritual truths within one's heart. Discovering this glorious truth of your true nature is the goal of yoga and all mystical philosophies.

Thus, in the same way as a form is within a stone and can be carved into a sculpture, all objects in creation exist, arise and dissolve into the primeval ocean. In other words, from the singular, preexistent ocean of consciousness arises all that exists as a thought in the mind of God, in the form of a Trinity or Triad of consciousness. Therefore, from the one arises the three.

The Self, God, is a sea of pure consciousness (Nu, Nun or Nunu), and out of that same sea came creation. Creation, then, is the sea which has been rippled with waves by the wind of thought vibrations. These thought vibrations are the result of desires of the mind. In the same way a placid lake reflects the unbroken image of the moon and when disturbed by a rock develops ripples, the pure consciousness of the mind is fragmented, rippled as it were, by the thought waves caused by desire for worldly experiences. Because of this rippling of consciousness, there appears to be many moons when there is in reality only one. If the lake of the mind were to be calmed, if there were no desires, then the mind would reflect its essential unity and non-duality. The primeval waters never changed into creation. Creation is the primeval waters itself and is continuously changing according to the winds of Cosmic vibration as prescribed by the Cosmic Mind (God). Therefore, creation is a continuous process which occurs at every moment by God's consciousness, i.e. God's very presence.

All matter is in reality cosmic mental thought substance in varying degrees of vibration and varying degrees of subtlety. The subtlest material is the Self, God, and the Self permeates all other things from the less subtle material which composes the astral world (Duat) to the grosser material which composes the physical world. Nevertheless, all matter is in a state of vibration and its existence is continually being sustained by the Self. This process of sustaining creation occurs every instant of every day just as the form and structure of the human body is sustained by a continuous process of new cells being created to substitute for those which are dying off. Every cell in the body is changed every year. Therefore, you do not have the same body you had a year ago. In the same way, the atoms of the house you live in are not the same as they were yesterday even though the house "looks" to be the same as before. Thus, what is considered to be "solid" matter is not solid at all. This is also the reason why things break down. If you were to allow a longer time to pass, say fifty years, this process would be more obvious. No object escapes the power of time which withers everything away. Sooner or later, everything breaks down and dissolves back into its original state. Even the most spectacular monuments and architectural creations will someday deteriorate to the point of no longer being usable or recognizable. Look at the Pyramids and the Sphinx. Having withstood the ravages of time for over 12,000 years, they are showing signs of deterioration. Even the most perfectly constructed machines or objects cannot escape the movement of time and eventually breaks down.

Think of a building. What is its life span? Say that it will last one hundred years and then will have to be torn down to build a new one. Every year there is a certain amount of destruction or dissolution which occurs in the atoms of the building. It could be said that it breaks down one hundredth of its life span every year. The movement of dissolution is slow, and those who do not reflect on it, those who do not acknowledge the hidden mystical teaching are missing the opportunity to discover the hidden essence which underlies the phenomenal world of time and space. You must study and understand the teachings of mystical spirituality now while there is "time," prior to the time of your death.

Another important teaching to understand about "matter" is that the substratum of all objects is the same and therefore, all objects can be transmuted or transformed into others. Even the most foul smelling rotten matter can be rearranged at the molecular or subatomic level and changed into the most fragrant substance. Solid matter can be converted into energy and then back into solid material form once again. These findings have been confirmed by modern physics experiments.

The underlying power of time comes from the continuous process of movement in creation. In the same manner that the human mind does not "stand still," the universe is continuous motion. Even at subatomic levels, matter, regardless of how solid it may appear to be, changes. The physical universe is in constant dissolution and creation. This is the reason why the solar and lunar barque of Amun-Ra (☉) traverses the heavens perpetually, and must constantly battle the forces of chaos and disorder (Set). Amun-Ra constantly establishes Maat (cosmic order) and thereby maintains the phenomenal universe in existence. The barque traverses through the heavens, and every evening is consumed by the cow-goddess, Nut. Every morning she gives birth to it, renewing its life.

This utterance is the progenitor of the Christian and Hebrew idea of creation described in the book of Genesis where God or the Spirit hovers over and stirs the primeval waters. The original Biblical texts express the creation more in terms of an act of sexual union: *Elohim* (Ancient Hebrew for gods/goddesses) impregnates the primeval waters with *ruach,* a Hebrew word which means *spirit, wind* or the verb *to hover*. The same word means *to brood* in Syriac. Thus, as the book of Genesis explains, creation began as the spirit of God moved over the waters and agitated those waters into a state of movement. In Western traditions, the active role of Divinity has been assigned to the male gender while the passive (receiving) role has been assigned to the female gender. This movement constitutes the dynamic *female* aspect of the Divine in Tantric (Eastern and African) terms while the potential-passive aspect is male. Creation is therefore understood to be a product of the interaction between these two aspects of the same reality: spirit (male) and primeval waters (female).

Since God is all that exists, then God is also the spirit and the primeval waters at the same time. Therefore, God interacts with himself/herself and emanates creation out of himself/herself. So within this teaching of the Bible lies the idea that creation and God are one and the same in a mysterious unexplained way. Some important questions arise here. If the Spirit is God and the primeval waters of creation are also God, then what is creation and where is the *Kingdom of Heaven?* Is creation separate from God or is creation held in the palm of God's hand? Where is God? Where did God come from? What is our relationship to God?, and so forth. What does this all mean? The study of Ancient Egyptian and Indian creation stories provides answers to these questions.

The Ancient Egyptian and Indian creation stories originate in the far reaches of antiquity, 5500 BCE and 3000 BCE respectively. The primeval Egyptian creation myth is similar in many respects to the creation story from the Indian mythology associated with the *Laws of Manu*. God felt desire. Wishing to create all things from his own body, God created the primeval waters from which all creation emerges. In the Bhagavad Gita, Lord Krishna* reiterates the wisdom of the primeval waters as he proclaims that he is the same Supreme Being who arose and formed creation. *As in the Ancient Egyptian pantheon of gods, all gods represent the Supreme Divinity, therefore Krishna and Narayana are manifestations of the same Self. In the Vibhuti Chapter of the Gita text Lord Krishna explains that among all Created things He is the foremost essence in all. The following verse is of keen interest in our study.

> 27. Among the horses know Me to be Uchhaihshrava that arose during the
> churning of the ocean; I am Airavata among the elephants, and the King among
> human beings.

Bhagavad Gita: Chapter 10

The teaching of the primeval ocean points to another mystical implication. The mind is like a lake of consciousness which is being buffeted by the winds of thoughts which have their origins in the feelings of desire, greed, hatred, anger, fear, attachment, elation, sorrow and impatience which are constantly blowing across its surface, creating waves of agitation and distractions in the mind. If these waves were to be calmed, if it were possible to make the mind free of the waves of desires, it would be possible to have clear insight into the depths of one's consciousness, just as it would be possible to see the bottom of a lake if it is free of waves. A most important task of every spiritual aspirant is to train the mind so that it not affected by the winds of emotion, desire and thoughts based on ignorance. When this practice is perfected, equanimity arises in the mind. This equanimity allows you to discover the depths of the lake of the mind and the Self within. In order to practice this teaching, it is necessary to have a keen understanding of the mystical nature of the universe and of one's own being. Then it is necessary that you live your life according to these teachings and remain mindful of every thought and emotion that enters your mind, rejecting those which are contrary to Maat (order, righteousness, truth) and accepting those that are in line with Maat.

From a yogic perspective, when you act with reason and uphold justice, correctness and virtue in your life, you are living in accord with Maat, and when you live in harmony with Maat, you are moving into harmony with the entire universe, God. When you live according to the whims, desires and feelings of the mind which are based on ignorance, anger, greed, fear, hatred and so on, you are living according to chaos and mental agitation. This is known as a hellish existence. Therefore, you must strive to cultivate peace, harmony and love toward humanity and the universe within your heart. These qualities will lead you to discover and experience the deeper essence of your being just as a swimmer dives below the waves and discovers the depths of the ocean. In the same way, you can dive below the waves of mental agitation (ignorance, anger, greed, fear, hatred, etc.) and discover the ocean-like Divine Self within you.

Perhaps the most important teaching to be derived from the primeval ocean is in reference to its fullness. As a metaphor for consciousness, which holds within itself infinite possibilities for expression as the universe, the primeval ocean is said to be "full." This "fullness" implies that it is complete, in much the same way as you are complete, even as entire dream worlds arise from your mind during sleep. The dream world is apparently "full" also. It seems to contain all of the necessary elements of a "real" world wherein there are people, objects, situations and you, as a subject who assumes various identities. Nevertheless, you are the real support of your dream. Its basis lies within your consciousness. In the same way, this entire universe lies within the consciousness of God who is the substratum of this entire creation, just as you are the substratum of your dreams. This teaching of the fullness of the primeval ocean is to be found in the *Book of Coming Forth By Day* (xvii. 76,79; lxxi. 13; cxxiv. 17. See the section entitled: The Goddess Aspect of Creation for the verse.)

The primeval waters is a metaphor to explain that all creation originally had no name or form. It is human beings who have named things and who have discerned forms in nature. In reality there are no names or forms in nature. Does a mountain know and call itself "mountain"? Does a bird in the sky say, "I am a bird and I have appendages called wings with which to fly"? Does a fish say, " I am a fish and I belong to species so and so? Does a dog say "I am an animal called dog and I am pedigree, so I am well-bred and you must look up to me," and so on? No, it is human beings, through the natural process, who have created all of these distinctions and all of the details that pertain to them. Nature does not call itself by any name nor does it define its existence by any accomplishment. It does not say, "I must grow plants or else I am a disgrace." The sun does not say, "I am unworthy because the clouds are blocking my light."

Modern science has proven that all *matter,* though appearing in a myriad of different colors and textures, is in reality one substance. Therefore, the perceptions of the human senses are illusory and deceptive.

People assign a value to their possessions and activities but all of these assignments are in reality illusions of the mind. They are illusions because they are not abiding realities. Someone who was popular at one time is not popular in another, etc. Also, people create their own goals and aspirations which they hope will bring happiness and fulfillment to their lives. However, they inevitably suffer the disappointments and frustration of unfulfilled desires, not understanding that they, like nature, do not need to "do" something in order to be happy or feel worthy. The problem is that people do not treat their disappointments as disillusionments. Rather, people dupe themselves into believing that "if they only try harder" or "get more money" or "find the right person" or "get that object that everyone else wants," etc. that they will indeed be able to discover true happiness. However, through countless incarnations you have experienced riches and poverty, exaltation and degradation, many times over. You have also experienced life as both male and female, and yet you have not discovered that which is truly fulfilling to your soul. Therefore, as long as you choose to continue to live in an egoistic manner, you should not expect that it will occur in the future either. Rather, apply yourself to learning the teachings of mystical spirituality (Yoga, Maat), and thereby discover what is truly abiding within your heart.

The Duat

The Ancient Egyptian concept of Creation includes three realms. These are the TA, ⎯⎯ ⵜ (Earth), Pet, ⎯⎯ ▢◠ (Heaven), and the Duat ★▧ (the Netherworld). The Duat is the abode of the gods, goddesses, spirits and souls. It is the realm where those who are evil or unrighteous are punished, but it is also where the righteous live in happiness. It is the "other world", the spirit realm. The Duat is also known as Amenta since it is the realm of Amen (Amun). The Duat is the realm Ra, as symbolized by the sun, traverses after reaching the western horizon, in other words, the movement of Ra between sunset and sunrise, i.e. at night. Some people thought that the Duat was under the earth since they saw Ra traverse downward, around the earth and emerged in the east, however, this interpretation is the understanding of the uninitiated masses. The esoteric wisdom about the Duat is that it is the realm of the unconscious human mind and at the same time, the realm of cosmic consciousness or the mind of God. Both the physical universe and the astral plane, the Duat, are parts of that cosmic consciousness.

The Duat represents Creation itself. As such it is composed of seven sections known as *Arits* or "Mansions". They may be thought of as rooms within rooms or dimensions within dimensions or planes of existence within successively higher planes of existence. These seven sections relate to the Seven Hathor Cows which are sired by Osiris in the form of Apis the *Bull of Amenti,* and they relate to the seven energy centers or levels of psycho-spiritual evolution of every human being, known as the *Serpent Power* or *Life Force Energy*. It is necessary to pass through all of these levels in order to reach the Supreme Abode. For this to be possible, the initiate must possess certain special knowledge about the passageways. Each passageway is guarded by a gatekeeper and a herald. They ask the initiate questions, and if answered correctly, they announce the new arrival and allow passage. The special knowledge consists of spiritual wisdom gained from the study of spiritual scriptures blended with meditative experience (the second and third levels of religious practice). Of course, spiritual studies and meditative experiences are only possible when life is lived according to virtuous principles (Maat).

There is a special realm within the Duat. This is the abode of Osiris as well as the ultimate destination of those who become enlightened. It is the realm of Supreme Peace. It is known as *Sekhet-Aaru,* or in other times, as *AmenDjed.* AmenDjed is a reference which unites the symbolism of Osiris with that of Amun (Amen) because *Djed,* ⌶, refers to the *Djed* or Djed Pillar of Osiris. The *Djed* symbolizes the awakened human soul which is well "established" in the knowledge of the Self. *Djedu,* ⌶⌶⊂⬭ ⊗, refers to the abode of Osiris. This is what the following line from the *Egyptian Book of Coming Forth By Day*, Chapter I: 13-15, is referring to:

nuk Djedi se Djedi au am - a em Djedu mesi - a Djedu
"I am steadfast, son of steadfast, conceived and born in the
region of steadfastness."

This special realm is shrouded in the deepest darkness and it is untouched by the myriad of cries, dismemberments and sufferings of unrighteous souls (the enemies of Ra) as well as the cries of happiness of the righteous souls who are experiencing heavenly or pleasurable conditions according to their good deeds of the past. This part of the Duat is composed of seven *Arits* or Halls. It transcends time and space as well as the mind and thoughts. It is absolute existence. The rest of the Duat as well as the physical world is relative reality. In this special realm, there is no growth of any kind. There is no birth, no death and no passage of time, just eternity. This is the meaning of the following hekau-utterance from *The Egyptian Book of Coming Forth By Day,* Chapter 125:1-17:

ANUNIAN THEOLOGY: THE MYSTICAL PHILOSOPHY OF RA RELIGION

The Osiris, the scribe Ani (initiate), whose word is truth, saith: "I have come unto thee. I have drawn close to you in order to experience thy beauties. My hands are extended in adoration of thy name of "MAAT" (Truth). I have come. I have drawn myself to the place where the cedar tree existeth not, where the acacia tree does not put forth shoots, and where the ground neither produces grass nor herbs. Now I have entered into the place of hidden things, and I hold converse with the god Set.... Osiris, the scribe Ani, has entered into the house into the House of Osiris, and he has seen the hidden and secret things which are therein....

That which is the place where nothing grows is the place of absolute stillness. It is a region that is devoid of forms or mental concepts of any kind. It is the primeval or celestial waters from which Creation arises. It is the place which is "hidden" from that which is in motion, the relative reality. Therefore, it is hidden to those whose minds are in constant motion due to desires, cravings, emotional attachments, greed, etc. That which is relative or temporal emanates out of that which is absolute and eternal. The relative reality emanates from this hidden place of stillness. It is to this place of stillness where one must go and have "communion" with God. When this occurs, that which is hidden is revealed.

This deepest and most dark realm of the Duat is Osiris, Himself, and this is why Osiris is referred to as the "Lord of the Perfect Black" and is often depicted as being black or green of hue. It is also why Nut, Isis, and Hathor are also described as "dark-skinned"*. They are emanations from this realm of blackness which is described as a void or *nothingness* in the hieroglyphic papyrus entitled *The Laments of Isis and Nephthys*. This notion of nothingness is akin to the Buddhist notion of *Shunya* or the "void", which refers to the area of consciousness which is devoid of mental concepts and thoughts. When there are no thoughts or forms in the mind, it is calm, expansive and peaceful. When there are thoughts in the mind, the mental awareness is narrowed and defined in terms of concepts. If the mind is confined to these concepts and narrow forms of thought, then it is confined to that which is limited and temporal. If it eradicates its desires, cravings and illusions, then it becomes aware of the innermost reality and realizes its connection to the entire cosmos. Thus, the teaching of the Duat (AmenDjed, Re-Stau, etc.) gives insight into the nature of the human mind. It is a description of the mental landscape, its demons (everything that leads to ignorance and mental agitation), and gods and goddesses (who represent the positive thoughts, feelings and the way to discover the abode of the innermost Self, everything that leads to peace, harmony and wisdom). Therefore, the task of a spiritual aspirant is to eradicate the concepts, agitation, desires and cravings in the mind and to discover the "hidden" innermost reality which is Hetep (Supreme Peace), eternal and pure. (*from an inscription in the temple of Denderah, Egypt)

From a higher level of understanding, the Duat is the unconscious mind and Osiris is that level which transcends the thinking processes... its deepest region. It is the level of consciousness that is experienced during deep dreamless sleep. Therefore, it is the "Hidden" aspect of the human heart, and thus, it is also known as Amun.

Neberdjer and The Origins of The Trinity of Creation

Picture 2: Neberdjer

"Nebertcher: Everything is Amun-Ra-Ptah, three in one."

—Ancient Egyptian Proverb

Picture 3: Amun-Ra-Ptah

Ancient Egyptian Mythology centered around the Creation of the universe out of a primeval ocean. This ocean was formless and homogenous. From this original essence, the Supreme Being arose in the form of an all-encompassing Supreme Being known as *Nebertcher* (All-encompassing existence) or *Pa Neter* (The Supreme Being). Nebertcher is an androgynous, formless being. However, Nebertcher received many symbolic names and forms throughout the vast Ancient Egyptian history. Nebertcher, also known as *Pa Neter* or "The God," distinguishing the Supreme Divinity from the neters, the gods and goddesses, which symbolizes cosmic powers through which the Supreme Being manifests. Many forms were associated with the Supreme Divinity. These included both male and female forms. Thus, the Ancient Egyptian gods, Osiris and Amun, who were male, were also known as Nebertcher. The Ancient Egyptian cow goddess, Mehurt, was also known as Nebertcher, the source of creation. In order to engender Creation, Nebertcher transformed into a Trinity, Amun-Ra-Ptah. This signifies that from a self-existent, singular and formless mass (Nu, the primeval ocean) the phenomenal universe consisting of objects with forms that have been given names, arises. For our study, we will use the words Supreme Divinity, Supreme Being, Pa Neter, Nebertcher, God, Divine Self, and The Self, interchangeably, to refer to the same Supreme Spirit.

The teaching of Nebertcher: Amun-Ra-Ptah is a profound study of mystical philosophy which encompasses the nature of Creation, Divinity and the origins and destiny of human life. It involves a study of the very makeup of the human heart (consciousness) and the way towards realizing the greatest goal of human existence. Thus, to believe that Ancient Egyptian Mythology and Mystical Religion is merely a fictitious yarn about some mythical characters is to entirely miss a most important teaching about the purpose of human life and the supreme goal of human existence, Spiritual Enlightenment, the discovery of the nature of God.

Above: The Great Trinity of Ancient Egypt including both male and female principles. A-Amun and Amenit or Amunet (Mut), B- Ra and Rai, C- Ptah and Sekhmet.

Ancient Egyptian Religion developed over a period of tens of thousands of years. Each segment of the four-fold system of mystical philosophy (Nebertcher, Amun, Ra, Ptah) in Ancient Egyptian Theban Religion as it is known today, originates in the Ancient Egyptian city of *Anu*, known to the Ancient Greeks as Heliopolis or the city of the sun. The presiding symbol of the Supreme Divinity was known there as *Ra*.

Neberdjer and The Creative Process

In the creation story involving the Ausarian Mysteries, Osiris assumes the role of Khepera and Tem:

"Neb-er-tcher saith, I am the creator of what hath come into being, and I myself came into being under the form of the god Khepera, and I came into being in primeval time. I had union with my hand, and I embraced my shadow in a love embrace; I poured seed into my own mouth, and I sent forth from myself issue in the form of the gods Shu and Tefnut." "I came into being in the form of Khepera, and I was the creator of what came into being, I formed myself out of the primeval matter, and I formed myself in the primeval matter. My name is Ausares (Osiris).

I was alone, for the gods and goddesses were not yet born, and I had emitted from myself neither Shu nor Tefnut. I brought into my own mouth, *hekau*, and I forthwith came into being under the form of things which were created under the form of Khepera."

Neb-er-tcher

These passages all point to the fact that while the name of the Supreme Being has changed under the different priesthoods, these are merely different expressions of the same principles and teachings which even use the same wording, therefore, there is no discontinuity or confusion within the theology. More importantly, the last passage reminds us that all of the names and forms are merely outward expressions of the Supreme Being, *Neb-er-tcher,* in its physical manifestation. Nebertcher who signifies the all-encompassing being is the source of the Trinity. Nebertcher includes all male and female aspects of the Trinity and is therefore to be understood as the androgynous and primordial being from which arose all names and forms, all gods and goddesses, all creation.

The other important point in this passage is that Osiris states that he brought himself, and thereby creation, into being by the just uttering his own name. The idea of the primeval utterance which emerges out of the hidden regions of existence and into the realm of time and space is taken up here by the priests of Osiris.

The Trinity and the Origins of the Gods and Goddesses

In the Ancient Egyptian Hymns of Amun, verse thirty two states that, *All the gods are three, Amun, Ra and Ptah, and there are none other like unto them.* This utterance commences the most important teaching of the hymn which will be elaborated in the next four utterances. Here you begin to discover *The Secrets of Sheti,* ⟨hieroglyphs⟩, Sheti means: *Spiritual discipline or program, to go deeply into the mysteries, to study the mystery teachings and literature profoundly, to penetrate the mysteries.* Recall the teaching:

⟨hieroglyphs⟩

"I became from God one gods three."

The Sheti which will be revealed here refers to the nature of the Trinity itself and the nature and origin of the n neters or gods and goddesses who compose Creation. This utterance points to the fact that all of the various gods and goddesses that are described in the varied religious scriptures are in reality manifestations of the same Trinity principle, which is of course, a manifestation of the One and Absolute Supreme Being. There is no other being besides the Supreme Divinity. Also, since everything is a manifestation of the Self, all things, including gods and goddesses (neters), planets, animals, stars, etc., are manifestations of the Trinity. This teaching emulates the one which is given in Memphite Theology (based on the God Ptah) as well as Anunian Theology (based on the God Ra) and closely follows another utterance from the *Egyptian Book of Coming Forth By Day,* Chap. 83 Lines 1-3:

> *I came into being from unformed matter, I came into existence as Khepera, I grew in the form of plants, I am hidden in the Tortoise. I am the essence of every god. I am yesterday...*

The Anunian Goddesses Aspect of the Supreme Being in the form of the God Ra

Picture 4: Goddess Rat

In the Anunian Theology ascribes one goddess as counterpart to the Supreme Divinity, Ra .

In Anunian theology the god Ra is accompanied by one goddess. Her name is *Rat* , and she is essentially the complementary counterpart to Ra.

In her name of Rat Tawi she represents the complementary opposite since Tawi means "the lands." This means that Rat is the physical universe and Ra is the Akhu or spirit.

She is also known as "Rat Tawi, the Mistress of the Gods and goddesses." Thus, Rat is actually the High Goddess, aspect of Ra, who manifests the female nature in juxtaposition to Ra's male nature.

Ra and *Ra Tawi*

This teaching is of course the fundamental principle of opposites wherein the God is understood as Spirit while the female is understood as Nature. Further, all opposite principles are also here implied. For example: above-below, movement-sedentary nature, magnetic-electric, you-me, here-there, etc. This teaching is descended from the philosophy of Heru and Herut (Hetheru).

or **Heru - Ancient name spelled out**

or **Herut - female aspect or form of ancient Heru**

The Cycles of Creation

Time and space are not real. They are in reality projections of the mind in and through the Trinity which is a metaphor to explain the triad of consciousness as previously discussed. However, it must be clearly understood that the entire creation, that is, every element of the triad of seer (Amun), seen (Ptah) and sight-mind (Ra), are in reality projections or emanations of the transcendental Self (Nebertcher). This projection is at all times existing in and supported by the Self; it has no independent reality or existence. Just as the projection of a dream world in the human mind is supported by the individual, the projection of the universe is supported by the cosmic mind (God). Thus, the world expresses as a triad (The Self or Spirit-Mind-Creation) which is a product of the underlying principle of duality (The Self and Creation-multiplicity of objects).

The findings of modern science have corroborated the mystical teachings of Ancient Egypt and India. In both of these cosmological systems Creation and time are understood as being circular or cyclical. This means that time moves in a circle rather than in a line from point A to point B as it is usually conceptualized in modern society. Modern science has shown that two lines moving in opposite directions join in infinity. This seems like a contradiction or paradox. However, upon reflection, the mystical wisdom of the ancients sheds light on this great truth.

In the epic Ancient Egyptian story known as "The Destruction of Evil Men and Women" there is a passage where the God Ra decides to leave the earth because as he explains, he will not be regenerated until the next period or cycle of Creation begins:

> "And the Majesty of this God (Ra) said unto the Majesty of Nu, "My members are weak and have suffered pain since primeval time, and I shall not recover until another period comes"."

The "period" referred to above is related to the cycle of Creation in which Ra emerges from the primeval waters and emanates Creation in the form of the Ennead. This implies that Creation has not occurred once but countless times. Creation is a cycle in which there is emergence and expansion which in human terms occurs over a period of billions of years, while from the perspective of God it occurs in a moment. From the Ancient Egyptian Pert Em Heru we receive the following wisdom:

What is the duration of life?

It has been decreed for millions of millions of duration. It is given to me to send the old ones. After that period of time I am going to destroy all created things. It is the earth that came forth from Nun, now coming forth into its former state.

We clearly are to understand that creation occurs in a cycle and not in a linear fashion with a set beginning and end. Life therefore is also not linear. It recurs in cycles. We are not finite and neither is the universe. It has existed always in manifest and unmanifest forms in accordance with God's will in the form of cycles of creation and dissolution like a human being's dreaming, waking up, dreaming again and waking and so on. It is interesting to note here that the Hindu system of reckoning time envisions time as a cyclical movement instead of as a linear. It involves cycles of Creation which evolves over a period of millions of years and ends up where they began. These units of time are called Yugas. This system of regarding time as a recurring cycle as in a circle is similar to the Ancient Egyptian system described above. Along with this, a correlation may be made between the Hindu God *Rama* and the Ancient Egyptian God *Ra.* In

Indian Mythology the Supreme Being, known as Brahman or "The Absolute", becomes three creative principles. These principles are known as the Trinity of *Brahma*, *Vishnu* and *Shiva*. Vishnu is said to incarnate from time to time in order to sustain *Dharma* or righteousness. Like the Ancient Egyptian *MAAT*, Dharma represents, order, righteousness and justice. When chaos in the form of evil and unrighteousness threaten to destroy society, God incarnates in human form in order to show humanity the proper way to live. Vishnu has had many incarnations. Two of the most popular ones are Krishna and Rama. This is the concept of Avatarism and it is also to be found in Ancient Egypt with the incarnation of Osiris and Isis as well as the incarnation of Hathor.

God is described as the one in whom "things have the beginning of their increase and of their decrease, and into whom they cease again." This means that creation itself, the entire universe, emanates from God and at the end of time the universe recedes back into God in much the same way as a wave rises out of the ocean and then recedes back into it again. In human life this process is more evident because the life-span of a human being is shorter than that of the universe, but nevertheless, they are the same. This point is also referred to in the Ancient Egyptian proverb: *"Soul to heaven, body to earth."*

The Psychospiritual Journey Through The Principles of Creation

Every human being is on a psycho-spiritual journey. They are in various ways trying to discover happiness, peace and fulfillment. Most people search in the world for these coveted goals. However, invariably they can only find limited fulfillment at best and in the end all of a person' achievements, no matter how grand, are relinquished by them at the time of death. Yoga philosophy shows that people are really searching for a deeper happiness and that if they were to understand how to pursue it their worldly desires, actions and experiences would be directed towards an inner spiritual discovery. The fruit of this inner journey is the discovery that one has infinite peace and bliss within and this is the true goal of life.

Picture 5: The Main Company of Gods and Goddesses

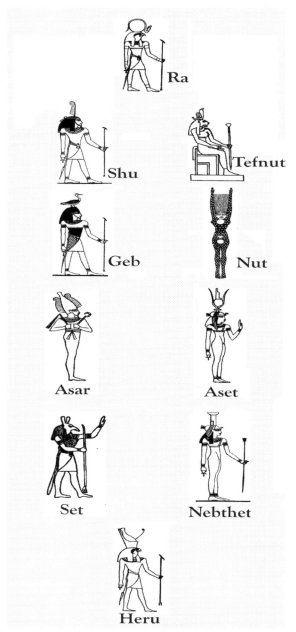

In order to successfully complete the journey everyone needs to evolve spiritually. So the characters of the myth of Creation and their various forms of interaction with each other are in reality an elaborate mystic code relating to the areas of human consciousness which need to be developed in order to grow spiritually. The first thing that is noticed when the deities of the Ancient Egyptian Creation, based on the teachings of Anu, are placed in a hierarchical fashion based on their order of Creation by Ra (see Picture above) is that they arise in accordance with their level of density. Density here refers to their order of subtlety of the elements in Creation. Ra is the first principle which emerges out of the Primeval Waters. He is the subtle, singular principle of Creation, the focus oneness in time and space. The ocean itself transcends time and space and is beyond existence and non-existence. Ra is the first principle to emerge out of the Absolute and his emergence signifies the beginning of existence.

The second important idea derived from the Pauti is that they represent a whole number, 10, and thus convey the idea of a special symmetry. The highest level, Ra, is juxtaposed with the lower level of the Pauti with the image of Heru. So at one end we see the perfect singularity of the Supreme Self and at the other we see the perfect combination of Spirit and Matter in the form of Heru. So while the figure above may be understood as a reference to a "higher" and a "lower" idea in reality the figure is not to be understood as a teaching of something that is above or better and something that is below or lesser. It is a teaching which expresses the essence of Creation, containing subtle as well as grosser objects which all emanate from the same source. The Ancient Egyptian teaching states that that which is above is the same as that which is below. If the Above and Below teaching is to be applied it should be understood as referring to the idea that everything in Creation is a reflection of the spiritual essence which transcends physicality. The physical universe is an emanation from the spiritual essence and as such is sustained by it. The very matter which constitutes Creation is in reality spirit in a condensed form just as when a person falls asleep their dream world is condensed out of their own consciousness. Nun is the underlying primordial consciousness of Creation. Ra may be seen as the Soul of Creation and Djehuti may be seen as the Cosmic Mind of Creation, Hetheru may be seen as the Vital Life Force of Creation and Maat may be seen as the underlying order of Creation. Djehuti, Hetheru and Maat are the underlying principles which sustain the Pauti.

Picture 6:

The Picture above displays the Pauti of Creation along with the underlying principles which sustain them. As explained earlier, the Pauti refers to Creation itself. The deities of the Pauti are nine in number and include Shu, Tefnut, Geb, Nut, Asar, Aset, Set, Nebthet and Heru. Maati, Hetheru and Djehuti are not part of the Pauti itself. They are subtle principles which support its existence. Anubis is a production of Spirit and mortal life. So he is a new principle emanating from Creation itself.

Picture 7: The boat of Ra with the Company of Gods and Goddesses

A Detailed Study of the Word Pa and its Derivatives

A-

Pa- demonstrative, this, the, to exist

B-

Pau - Primeval Divinity- The Existing One

C-

Paut- Primeval time - remote ages-beginning time

D-

Paut- stuff, matter, substance, components which make something up.

E-

Pauti- The Primeval God; Primeval Divinity who is self-Created; Dual form relates to rulership of Upper and Lower Egypt

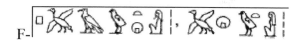

F-

Pauti-u- Primeval Divinity with male or female determinative - source of all multiplicity in Creation.

G-

Pat (paut) **n Neteru-** Company of gods and goddesses

H-

Pauti- Company of nine gods and goddesses

I-

Pau or **Paut** -human beings, me, women

The Ancient Egyptian words and symbols related to the Company of Gods and Goddesses (Pauti) indicate several important mystical teachings. The root of the Ancient Egyptian word Pauti is *pa* (Picture A). Pa means "to exist." Thus, Creation is endowed with the quality of existence as opposed to non-existence. *Pau* (Picture B) is the next progression in the word. It means the *Primeval Divinity*, the source of Creation. *Paut* (Picture C and D) is the next evolution of the word, Pau, meaning *primeval time* and *the very substance out of which everything is created is the one and the same*. *Pauti* is the next expression of **pa** and it has two major meanings. It refers to the *Primeval Divinity* or Divine Self (God) (Picture E). *Pautiu* refers to *Pauti* but in plural, as well as being a gender specific term implying, *the Divinity as the source of the multiplicity in creation*. In the Ancient Egyptian language, like Spanish for example, all objects are assigned gender. Also, Pauti refers to the deities who comprise the *Company of Gods and Goddesses* (Picture G and H). *Paut* (men) or *Pautet* (women) also refers to *living beings*, especially *human beings* (Picture I).

Pa ➔   Pau ➔   Paut ➔   Pauti ➔   Pautiu ➔   Paut and Pautet

Therefore, the most important teaching relating to the nature of Creation is being given here. The gods and goddesses of the creation are not separate principles or entities. They are in reality one and the same as the Primeval Divinity. They are expressions of that Divine Self. However, they are not transformation from or evolutions from the Divine Self, but the very same Divine Self expressing as Creation. So even though God is referred to as a primordial deity who did something a long time ago or set into motion various things, in reality God and Creation are one and the same. Ra is the God of primeval time as well as the gods and goddesses of Creation which sustain it all the time. With this understanding it is clear to see that God is not distant and aloof, observing Creation from afar. The Divine Self is the very basis of Creation and is in every part of it at all times. This is why the terms *Pa-Neter* and *neteru* are also used to describe the Divine. Pa-Neter means "The Supreme Being" and neteru means "the gods and goddesses." Also, the word "neteru" refers to creation itself. So neter-u emanates from Neter. Creation is nothing but God who has assumed various forms or neteru: trees, cake, bread, human beings, metal, air, fire, water, animals, planets, space, electricity, etc. This is a profound teaching which should be reflected upon constantly so that the mind may become enlightened to its deeper meaning and thereby discover the Divinity in nature.

The Divine Self is not only in Creation but is the very essence of every human being as well. Therefore, the substratum of every human being is in reality God as well. The task of spiritual practice and Yoga is to discover this essential nature within your own heart. This can occur if one reflects upon this teaching and realizes its meaning by discovering its reality in the deepest recesses of one's own experience. When this occurs the person who has attained this level of self-discovery is referred to as having become enlightened. They have discovered their true, divine nature. They have discovered their oneness with the Divine Self.

In conclusion, it must be understood that Kemetic language is synonymous with Kemetic philosophy. As such, when talking one must adhere to truth. The ultimate truth is that when speaking of objects we are in reality speaking about principles whose deeper basis is the Divine Self. When words are spoken they immediately take on the first level of reality as they engender an image in the mind of the listener. When a listener acts upon listening, the speech takes on a reality in the physical plane. Therefore, the speech is a reflection of an idea, a concept and physical reality is a reflection of speech. The cause underlying the concept is the real name of a thing, its higher reality and this essence has no name or form in its potentiality but only in its relative manifestation. This relative manifestation is the world of time and space and all living and non-living objects in it. Therefore, we have three levels of reality, the thought, the word and the actual object existing in the physical world. However, these are only relative realities since they are all ephemeral in nature and not abiding. The creative essence (God-transcendental consciousness) which gave power to the thought, the concept, is the source and substratum which lends temporary reality to the projection (thought, the word and the actual object).

The Divinities and their Metaphysical Significance

Picture 8: The Tree of Gods and Goddesses of Anunian Theology

Hetheru-Djehuti-Maat

Hetheru, Djehuti, and Maat are special cases. They are not part of the tree of gods and goddesses and yet they are emanations of Ra and they fulfill an essential role in Anunian Theology. They constitute subtle principles, subtler than the divinities of the tree of Gods and Goddesses. As such they form the essential basis of Creation, as its very matrix. Through them the grosser divinities and their activities as well as those of human beings becomes possible.

Picture 9: The Divinities Maat, Hetheru and Djehuti

Picture 10: Hetheru (Het-hor, Hathor)

The Hieroglyphic symbol, [symbol], for the name of the goddess means [symbol], *Het (house) and Heru,* [symbol], *(the god of light).*

In a text from the Temple at Dier al-Medina, Hetheru is referred to as having the same divine attributes as Heru. She is described as *The Golden One* and *The Queen of the Gods.* Her shrines are even more numerous than those of Heru. Hetheru or Het-Heru, meaning *The House of Heru* or *The House Above* (heavens), became identified, like Heru, with the salvation of the initiate. In the *Egyptian Prt m Hru,* she is the one who urges the initiate to do battle with the monster *Apep,* the symbol of egoism which spurs negativity and evil, so as not to lose {his/her} heart as she cries out: "Take your armor." In a separate papyrus, the initiate is told that she (Hetheru) is the one who "will make your face perfect among the gods and goddesses; she will open your eye so that you may see every day... she will make your legs able to walk with ease in the Netherworld, Her name is Hetheru, Lady of Amenta."

More forms of Hetheru

In Chapter 24, the role of Hetheru in the process of salvation is specified as the initiate speaks the words which will help {him/her} become as a lotus:

"I am the lotus, pure, coming forth out into the day. I am the guardian of the nostril of Ra and keeper of the nose of Hetheru. I make, I come, and I seek after he, that is Heru. I am pure going out from the field."

The lotus has been used since ancient times to symbolize the detachment and dispassion that a spiritual aspirant must develop. The lotus emerges everyday out of the murky waters of the pond in order to receive the rays of the sun. The spiritual aspirant, a follower of the goddess, must rise above egoism and negativity (anger, hatred, greed, and ignorance) in life in order to gain in wisdom and spiritual enlightenment. Hetheru and Heru form a composite archetype, a savior with all of the complementary qualities of the male and female principles, inseparable, complete and androgynous.

Hetheru represents the power of Ra, the Supreme Spirit, therefore, associating with her implies coming into contact with the boundless source of energy which sustains the universe. Therefore, making contact with Hetheru implies developing inner will power and vitality which engenders clarity of vision that will lead to the discovery of what is righteous and what is unrighteous. A mind which is constantly distracted and beset with fetters (anger, hatred, greed, conceit, covetousness, lust, selfishness, etc.) cannot discern the optimal course in life. It becomes weak willed because the negative emotions and feelings drain the mental energy. Thus, unrighteous actions and sinful thoughts arise and the weak mind cannot resist them. Unrighteous actions lead to adverse situations and adverse situations lead to pain and sorrow in life. In this sense Hetheru comes to human beings in the form of adversities to urge them to reflect on their unrighteous actions and challenge them to sublimate their ego. However, those who are not very reflective might view it as punishment, since they do not have a higher philosophical understanding.

Picture 11: Goddess Maat

Order, Righteousness, Justice, Balance, Harmony, Truth

"Those who live today will die tomorrow, those who die tomorrow will be born again;
Those who live Maat will not die."

Who is Maat?

Maat is one of the most important divinities in respect to the promotion of the spiritual evolution of an aspirant. Even though the figure of goddess Maat is not usually seen in the *Rau Prt m Hru,* her presence is the most strongly felt of all. Her name is mentioned more than any other goddess and indeed, she is said to be an aspect of the all-goddess, Aset. Therefore, in order to understand the *Prt m Hru,* we must have a working knowledge of the goddess and her philosophy. When Ra emerged in his Boat for the first time and creation came into being, he was standing on the pedestal of Maat. Thus the Creator, Ra, lives by Maat and has established Creation on Maat. Who is Maat? She is the divinity who manages the order of Creation. She is the fulcrum upon which the entire Creation and the Law of Cause and Effect or Karma, functions. Maat represents the very order which constitutes creation. Therefore, it is said that Ra created the universe by putting Maat in the place of chaos. So creation itself is Maat. Creation without order is chaos. Maat is a profound teaching in reference to the nature of creation and the manner in which human conduct should be cultivated. It refers to a deep understanding of Divinity and the manner in which virtuous qualities can be developed in the human heart so as to come closer to the Divine.

Maat is a philosophy, a spiritual symbol as well as a cosmic energy or force which pervades the entire universe. She is the symbolic embodiment of world order, justice, righteousness, correctness, harmony and peace. She is also known by her headdress composed of a feather which symbolizes the qualities just mentioned. She is a form of the Goddess Aset, who represents wisdom and spiritual awakening through balance and equanimity.

In Ancient Egypt, the judges and all those connected with the judicial system were initiated into the teachings of Maat. Thus, those who would discharge the laws and regulations of society were well trained in the ethical and spiritual-mystical values of life, fairness, justice and the responsibility to serve and promote harmony in society as well as the possibility for spiritual development in an atmosphere of freedom and peace, for only when there is justice and fairness in society can there be an abiding harmony and peace. Harmony and peace are necessary for the pursuit of true happiness and inner fulfillment in life.

Maat signifies *that which is straight*. Two of the symbols of Maat are the ostrich feather (𝄫) and the pedestal (▭) upon which God stands. The Supreme Being, in the form of the god *Atum*, *Asar*, and *Ptah,* are often depicted standing on the pedestal.

Maat is the daughter of Ra, the high God, thus in a hymn to Ra we find:

> *The land of Manu* (the West) *receives thee with satisfaction, and the goddess Maat embraces thee both at morn and at eve... the god Djehuti and the goddess Maat have written down thy daily course for thee every day...*

Another Hymn in the Papyrus of Qenna (Kenna) provides deeper insight into Maat. Qenna says:

> *I have come to thee, O Lord of the Gods, Temu-Heru-khuti, whom Maat directeth... Amen-Ra rests upon Maat... Ra lives by Maat... Asar carries along the earth in His train by Maat...*

Maat is the daughter of Ra, and she was with him on his celestial boat when he first emerged from the primeval waters along with his company of gods and goddesses. She is also known as the *Eye of Ra, Lady of heaven, Queen of the earth, Mistress of the Netherworld and the lady of the gods and goddesses.* Maat also has a dual form or *Maati.* In her capacity of God, Maat is *Shes Maat* which means *ceaseless-ness and regularity* of the course of the sun (i.e. the universe). In the form of Maati, she represents the South and the North which symbolize Upper and Lower Egypt as well as the Higher Self and lower self. Maat is the personification of justice and righteousness upon which God has created the universe, and Maat is also the essence of God and creation. Therefore, it is Maat who judges the soul when it arrives in the judgment hall of Maat. Sometimes Maat herself becomes the scales upon which the heart of the initiate is judged. Maat judges the heart (unconscious mind) of the initiate in an attempt to determine to what extent the heart has lived in accordance with Maat or truth, correctness, reality, genuineness, uprightness, righteousness, justice, steadfastness and the unalterable nature of creation.

Who is Maati?

Who are the Maati goddesses? In the segment above we introduced the idea of opposites in creation. The Hall of Maat, known as the hall of judgment for the heart, is presided over by two goddesses known as *Maati*.

Picture 12: The Two Maati goddesses preside over the judgment of the heart in the Prt m Hru

The goddesses Aset and Nebethet have a special relationship to the Maati goddesses. The Ancient Egyptian texts reveal that these two goddesses are none other than Aset and Nebethet. As stated earlier, Aset and Nebethet are depicted as looking exactly alike, the only difference being in their headdresses: Aset ⌋, Nebethet ⌶ or ⌸. However, the essential meaning of their symbols is inverted, that is, the goddesses are in reality just inverted images of each other. Thus, they are complementary goddess principles which operate to manifest life-death-life or the cycle of birth-death-rebirth known as reincarnation.

Sati merti arati nebti Maati
The two daughters, goddesses {Aset and Nebethet} of all righteousness and truth.

Aset and Nebethet are also known as *Rekhtti,* the two goddesses. They manifest in the Judgment hall of Maat in the *Egyptian Book of Coming Forth By Day* as *Maati* or the double Maat goddesses who watch over the weighing of the heart of the initiate (*The Asar*) in their name as *Sati merti arati nebti Maati.* Aset and Nebethet are the basis of the judgment of the soul and the criterion which decides its fate in life as well as after death.

Picture 13: Forms of Djehuti

Djehuti is the symbol of right reason, the link to the Higher Self. When the determination to pursue the Divine arises, the struggle becomes a holy war against ignorance and illusion within one's consciousness. If this process is not understood as a struggle to overcome anger, hatred, greed, bigotry, jealousy, etc., within one's self, the energy of the struggle becomes directed to the world outside of oneself in the form of political, religious, social, ethnic, gender, etc., conflicts.

The struggle between Heru and Set does not end with either destroying the other. Heru pursues the path of reason seeking counsel with the reasoning of Djehuti. Wisdom follows the exercise of reason, and reason follows the practice of studying, questioning, reflecting and inquiring into the nature of truth. Set, the lower self, refuses to abide by the decree of wisdom but he is eventually sublimated through his own humiliation and ignorance. In the end, when the aspirant is aligned with all the divine forces, the lower self can no longer struggle. The overwhelming force of the Divine pushes the lower self into a position of service rather than of mastership. This is its rightful place.

Djehuti also represents the moon. In this capacity he is also the minister of Ra. As the moon's light is a reflection of the Sun's light, so too the intellectual capacity of the mind is a reflection of spirit consciousness. To the extent that one is in touch with the spirit, to that extent one is able to exercise the higher intellect. Thus, Djehuti represents the intellectual capacity of every human being. He represents purity of thought and as such, all aspirants should engage in disciplines that promote purity of mind (acting with maat, study of spiritual scriptures, worship and meditation).

Shu and Tefnut

Next Ra gives rise to Shu and Tefnut. Shu is the principle of air and space. Space is the first thing necessary in order for Creation to be possible. In Eastern mystical teachings this principle is referred to as Ether. The next principle of Creation is Tefnut. She symbolizes the potential dynamic energy, the Life Force within all creation. She is that which allows creation to have movement. She is represented as a lioness and she is related to the Ancient Egyptian goddess known as Sekhmet. Sekhmet is the goddess who presides over Sekhem or the Serpent Power Life Force of all things.

Geb and Nut

Next Shu and Tefnut give rise to Geb and Nut. Geb and Nut are the earth and the heavens respectively. So, from the subtlest essence of Creation (Ra) the subtle principles, space and life force energy, emerged. Now from space and life force energy even more dense principles arise and these constitute the physical world, stars, planets, etc.

Thus, from Ra the basic principles of Creation emanated and this sets the stage for the existence of human beings and the life forms of Creation. Notice that all of the principles (Shu and Tefnut and Geb and Nut) are pairs of opposites which have been given male and female iconography. This points to the teaching that existence is a mingling of opposite principles which emanate from the single essence. However, in and of themselves they are not what constitutes life from the human point of view because they do not contain the dynamic consciousness of the Self or Spirit (Ra) in the proper manner to allow reasoning, feeling, etc. to manifest. Reasoning, feeling, memory, action, love and other capacities are what constitute human existence. In order for these to manifest, the proper combination of matter and spirit must be present.

Picture 14: Shu separates Geb and Nut

Above: The Goddess Nut stretches over and across the god Geb and Ra sails over Nut's body, creating and sustaining Creation.

After Ra Created heaven and earth (Geb and Nut) they loved each other so much that they engaged in perpetual lovemaking and remained locked in intercourse. Ra decreed that they should be separated so he ordered Shu (air-space-ether) to come between them and separate them. Nut had become pregnant and when Geb removed his penis (the obelisk) from her, she gave birth to the divinities that constitute the elements of human existence. Thus, the next five deities represent that melding of God and Creation (spirit and matter), which allows human life to exist and to be sustained. Asar is the soul; Aset is intuition (enlightenment); Set is ego consciousness; Nebethet is mortal nature and worldly consciousness; Heru ur is perfection, the balance of spirit and matter, the enlightened human being.

Asar and Aset, and Set and Nebthet

From Geb and Nut arise Asar and Aset. Asar and Aset represent the epitome of human existence. In the view of the myth Asar is seen as the soul of Creation, a reflection of the Divine consciousness (Ra). Aset represents intuitional knowledge, the wisdom which transcends time and space and is united with the soul.

Set and Nebthet represent the lower nature of every human being. Set is the egoistic will of a human being, that which is selfish, greedy, impulsive and full of desires for sensual pleasures. Therefore, Set is that aspect of a human being that is prone to becoming involved with the desires and egoistic tendencies of the mind. When this occurs a human being does not see things clearly and becomes enslaved as it were, by his or her own desires, emotions and attachments for worldly objects and for worldly experiences. This is known as spiritual ignorance or bondage to the world of time and space. It is also the cause of reincarnation or the cycle of birth and death which every human being suffers until they attain spiritual enlightenment.

Nebthet represents mortality and all that is transient in human existence. She is physical nature itself which transforms itself constantly, bringing forth life only to see it die and be reborn again. Thus, she also presides over reincarnation but also she represents another important principle of human existence. Nebthet is the quality of Devotion in all life which is expressed in its highest degree through the emotion of love which manifests in every human being. Love manifests in various degrees. Some people love themselves in a selfish way, caring form themselves alone. This condition is Set operating through them. Others love material objects and sense pleasures. This is also Setian although a more expanded manifestation of love. Others love family members and still others love their community. Love may expand to include one's country or even humanity. As the feeling of love expands a person loves the earth and the heavens and then the subtle essence which enlivens Creation itself (God). Thus, they grow in universal love and in so doing they are actually growing in cosmic consciousness because God is universal love itself, the cosmic expansion of love and devotion for all that exists.

Nebthet is the reflection of Aset. Her name means "Lady of the House." House here implies mortal or physical human existence whereas Aset represents the subtle spirit realm which transcends mortality. In any case they are one and the same goddess expressing in two forms, the subtle as well as the gross aspects of Creation in human consciousness. The fact that they are both consorts of Asar points to the fact that the Spirit (Asar) is wedded to the subtle (Aset) as well as the gross essence (Nebthet) of Creation. It is notable that while Nebthet is supposed to be the consort of Set she is nevertheless drawn to Asar. Set produces no offspring. In the same way, a life of vice, egoism and selfishness produces no offspring in the form of spiritual enlightenment, abiding joy, peace or happiness, but only frustration, unrest and discontent.

Heru and Hetheru

Hor or Horus (also known as Heru), is the epitome of all human qualities when they are sublimated, or harmonized. He is the offspring of the Spirit (Asar) and intuitional wisdom (Aset). When a human being evolves in consciousness to their full potential they become masters of their own consciousness as well as of their own physical nature. They are the perfect blend of matter and spirit, desire, devotion, wisdom and power. They transcend time and space even as they continue to live in time and space. Such a life is glorious and it is the goal of all human beings.

The goddess Hetheru is the subtle essence of spiritual power in Creation. She is also known as the Eye of Ra which is the sundisk. The sundisk is the ultimate symbol of the dynamic power of the Divine Self which sustains all life. Her name indicates a close relationship with Horus. The name "Het-hor" means *House of Hathor* (Het-ur, Het-Hor). Horus is indeed the one who dwells in the *House of Hathor* creation itself. Horus is none other than Ra in another form and Horus is also Djehuti. Horus is also Nefer-Tem. Nefer-Tem is the beautiful one arising from the primeval waters. Thus, every human being (Horus) is not separate from God but is essentially God, who arose from the primeval waters (Nefer-Tem). The Self manifests as the universe as well as the consciousness (Ra) and intelligence (Djehuti) which resides, lives and interacts within that creation.

Anpu (Anubis)

Anubis is the offspring of Spirit (Asar) and pure physical nature (Nebthet). Anubis is often related to the dog or jackal deity. The jackal deity has two aspects, *Anubis* and *Apuat.* Anubis is the embalmer, the one who prepares the initiate, the *Shti* (one who is in his coffin-the body). As a neophyte, the initiate is considered to be dead (a mummy) since he/she does not have conscious realization of the transcendental reality beyond the ego-personality. He or she is an ordinary mortal human being in consciousness. At this stage the aspirant must be prepared through virtue and physical purification to receive the teachings, because without this preparation, the highest teachings would fall on deaf ears. The next aspect is *Apuat, The opener of the Ways.* In this context Anubis represents vigilance and the constant practice of discrimination and watchfulness (mindfulness) over the ego-self. Apuat represents the development of intuitional realization which unfolds within the human heart in degrees. Gradually, through the practices of discrimination and watchfulness, the ego-self becomes effaced and reveals the true self as one with Osiris.

Anubis represents: "Control of the thoughts", "Control of one's actions", and "Devotion of purpose", "Learning how to distinguish between right and wrong," "Learning to distinguish the real from the unreal". Anubis is solely devoted to Osiris, and as such, represents the process of concentration and oneness of vision which lead to Divine awareness.

Anubis also implies dispassion and detachment from worldly desires. This should not be misinterpreted as a pathetic development. Detachment from the world implies a keen understanding that the world and all objects in it cannot bring happiness to the soul, because they are transient and fleeting. Since the essence of all objects is the Self, in detaching from objects you are merely detaching from the reflection of the Self and attaching to the real Self behind the objects. From the perspective of spirituality, the act of detaching from objects does not mean simply giving up objects. Rather, it means you now have a more profound way of seeing and understanding objects. You now have deeper insight into the true nature of the object; it is this understanding which allows you to detach from objects. You understand they are temporal creations from the source of all existence, your very own heart, as in a dream, and therefore are not abiding realities that can or should be possessed or owned.

The qualities of Anubis assist in the spiritual movement since an intellectual grasp of mystical philosophy is necessary for progress on the spiritual path. However, intellectual sophistication, sharpness and subtlety are only a means and not an end in itself. Spiritual evolution necessitates a transcendental movement beyond the level of the ordinary human intellect (the level of the mind and senses).

The Spiritual Journey To Enlightenment Based on the Pauti

The journey of spiritual enlightenment may be seen as a reverse of the creation process. In the creation everything emanates from the Nun or primordial ocean and expresses in the form elements in succeeding levels of denseness. These elements also manifest in the form of opposites which appear to be exclusive and separate from each other but which are in reality complements to each other. Therefore, the spiritual journey is based on first sublimating the ego and its desires which cause a person to become entrenched as it were in the physical realm of existence and to be oblivious to the higher planes of existence. Spiritual practice consists in developing the intellectual capacity by understanding the illusoriness of the opposites of Creation. This leads a spiritual aspirant to develop spiritual aspiration and the qualities to go beyond the appearances of nature and to discover the Absolute existence which is the real basis for all that exists.

Nun
(Discovering the absolute and transcendental essence which is beyond even the singularity of consciousness (Ra)- beyond time and space and the opposites of creation (Shu-Tefnut-Geb-Nut) as well as the concepts of existence or non-existence.)

↑

Ra-Tem
(Discovering the single essence which underlies the multiplicity of nature-Cosmic Consciousness.)

↑

Shu ⇔ Tefnut
(Discovering the more subtle aspects of nature.)

↑

Geb⇔Nut
(Discovering the gross aspects of nature.)

↑

Hetheru –Djehuti - Maat
(Spiritual Strength - Right Reasoning - Righteous Action
These higher spiritual qualities allow a spiritual aspirant to discover the mysteries of nature— to pierce the vail of illusion which prevents the discovery of the underlying essence of nature (Creation)—God.)

↑

Heru
(Advanced Spiritual Aspiration, having developed spiritual qualities such as purity, truthfulness, honesty, etc. to pursue a spiritual lifestyle which will lead to success in life as well as spiritual enlightenment—self-discovery.)

↑

Asar ⇔ Aset
(Glimpses of the transcendental Divine Gory and initiation into the teachings of mystical wisdom.)

↑

Apuat
(Intellect-understanding that the world is perishable and that there is something else which is abiding. Also, understanding the real meaning of life and the real goal of life—to attain enlightenment. Understanding what is real from what is unreal, truth from untruth.)

↑

Asar⇔Nebthet
(Devotion to the Divine - Faith in the existence of the Divine Self and in the idea that Enlightenment is a real possibility.)

↑

Set
(Sublimation of the ego and the lower self-control over the sex drive and the negative qualities such as anger, hatred, greed, covetousness, jealousy, etc.)

Classes of Divinities in Anunian Theology

There are four classes of divinities that can be discerned from Anunian Theology. First there is the Supreme being, that entity who is transcendental and inscrutable, from whence the next order of divinity arises. In this category we find Neberdjer and Net or Heru and Hetheru. In the next level we find the cosmic divinities, those who sustain Creation. In this group we find Ra, Shu, Tefnut, Geb and Nut. Next we encounter the human divinities. They compose the aspects of the human personality. These are Asar, Set, Aset, Nebethet and Heru-Ur.

The Principle of Creator and the Nine Divinities

Based on Anunian theology, as it is presented in the Ancient Egyptian Pyramid Texts and other Kemetic scriptures, the order, nomenclature and attributes of the Ancient Egyptian divinities of the Creation may be viewed as follows.

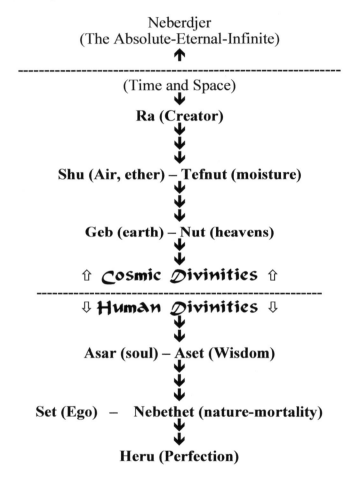

The Mystical Significance of Number In Creation

The Number 7

There is important mystical significance related to the number nine (9) within Ancient Egyptian mystical philosophy. The Company of gods and goddesses of Ptah (Nun, Nunet, Huh, Huhet, Kuk, Kuket, Amon, Amonet) total eight in number and with Ptah they add up to nine. In the Company of gods and goddesses of Ra (Ra-Tem, Shu, Tefnut, Geb, Nut, Set, Osiris, Isis, Nephthys, and Heru-ur) there is also a total of nine. The number nine is to be found in the very heart of Ancient Egyptian Mythology, the Cosmogony and Cosmogony itself, because the number nine is the basis of creation. This is why the number nine recurs in nature, in chemical and physics experiments. Creation unfolds into nine relative aspects and they are all rooted in and sustained by the Supreme Being, the first principle. This idea is mythologically expressed as the emergence from the primeval ocean and the eventual submergence back into the ocean at the end of time, thus creating a cyclical movement of the spirit wherein Creation is continually emanated (created), dissolved and re-emanated again. If the gods and goddesses of the Pautti are assigned numbers their qualities explain the numerological aspects of Creation and these explain the cosmogony of Creation.

$$
\begin{array}{c}
\text{Nun } (\infty) \\
\Downarrow \\
\text{Ra-Tem } (1) \\
\Downarrow \\
\text{Shu } (2) \quad \Leftrightarrow \quad \text{Tefnut } (3) \\
\Downarrow \\
\text{Geb } (4) \quad \Leftrightarrow \quad \text{Nut } (5) \\
\Downarrow \\
\text{Asar } (6) \quad \Leftrightarrow \quad \text{Aset } (7) \\
\Downarrow \\
\text{Set } (8) \quad \Leftrightarrow \quad \text{Nebthet } (9) \\
\Downarrow \\
\text{Heru } (10)
\end{array}
$$

The world is like a dream that arises during sleep. The dream seems to be very real and abiding ("full") but when you wake up you discover that it is of lesser value than what you believed previously. The dream was an emanation from you and it has no reality unless you dream it. The dream is the realm of numbers and you are infinity. You are the "fullness" which gives rise to your dream.

When the multiples of the number nine are added they all add up to 9. Also, every number that ads up to nine is divisible by 9. Thus, nine is the highest number. The Creator, the Supreme Being is in reality not part of the Creation and in absolute terms is not counted as one of the Neteru. The Supreme Being is the transcendental principle engendering Creation. Therefore, in mathematical terms, the Supreme Being is transcendental consciousness, i.e. infinity (∞). Nun is the infinite source material for Creation and Ra-Tem is the individuating principle emerging from the Nun. Nun and Ra-Tem are essentially aspects of the same Supreme Being. Creation is given value due to the presence of the Self who is the Absolute Reality which sustains Creation. However, considering the Supreme Being as number one, the principle of fullness, Heru-ur then becomes number ten. This is why in Ancient Egyptian Mystical Philosophy the number ten is special to Heru. Thus, Heru signifies fullness and completion in time and space while Ra relates to fullness transcending time and space. This is the original teaching whereby hermetic philosophy (latest version of Kemetic (Ancient Egyptian) Mystical Philosophy), and the even later Christianity, derive the teaching of "As Above, So Below" and "I am the Alpha and the Omega" respectively. Having discovered Shetau Akhet and your Higher Self as being one and the same, you have discovered all that there is to be known, you have achieved the number nine.

The Sacred Numbers of Creation and their Important Subsets

cht n ankh - tree of life

Left: Number Correspondences in the Divinities of Anunian Theology
Right: Tree of Life of Anunian Theology

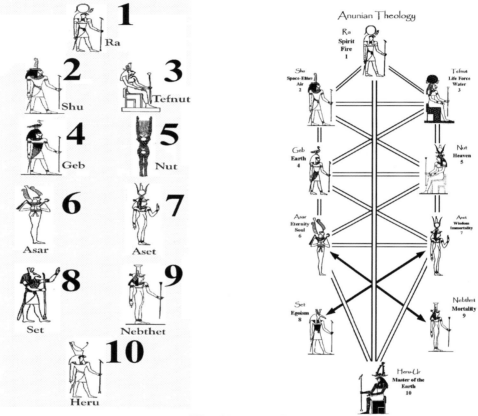

The Number 7

From the sacred numbers of the Pautti we are also given the number seven, the number of the goddess. The number seven relates to the seven aspects of Creation wherein human life has its manifestations. Ra has are seven *bas* or souls. The number seven related to the seven psycho-spiritual energy centers which sustain human life, the seven realms of existence as symbolized by the seven Hetheru goddesses, the seven notes in music, the seven colors of the rainbow, etc. There are certainly more notes in music, energy centers and colors beyond the perceptible range. However, the number seven denotes the perceptible range in which human existence has its mundane (typical of this world; secular) manifestation. Seven times seven gives us 42, the number of ancient Egyptian Nomes or primordial settlements which gave rise to Ancient Egypt. Forty two is also related to the number of main precepts in Maat Philosophy.

The Number 6

The number 6 was regarded by Pythagoras, an initiate of the Kemetic Mysteries, as the number of "full manifestation", the limit number. This idea is seen in music as the number six being the limiting factor of harmonies and there are only six harmonies in music. Thus, Asar, who symbolizes the soul, is fullness of manifestation of the spirit in time and space in the form of individual sparks of life that give rise to human beings. Put another way, each human being is like a wave in the ocean. The Supreme is the ocean and each soul is the limit of manifestation of that ocean as an individual. Therefore, the number six relates to

The Number 4

The number four is the number of Creation. Geb is the god of the Earth. Thus prayers are offered in a fourfold manner to the four cardinal points of the compass. This practice thereby fills Creation with the utterances and their vibrations.

The Number 3

From the seven we are reduced to the number three, the number of the Cosmic Trinity (Amun-Ra-Ptah) and of the Creation Trinity (Khepri-Ra-Tem). The Trinity relates to the modes of Consciousness (Seer-seen and sight or subject-object and interacting medium) and the modes of matter (Harmonious-Agitated-Sedentary). These principles govern the manifestations of consciousness as it differentiates into the various forms referred to as matter. Further, the number three relates to father, mother and child, past present and future, and in space: length, height and width. Thus, in Kemetic religious practice, prayers are offered thrice daily (morning, midday and evening). In musical philosophy, the number three is the number of manifestation. No more that three notes can be combined to make consonances. This means that even though there may be a duality present (Self and Other), all you have is a unison of two which is essentially equal to the original One. There still cannot be manifestation unless a third principle is present, i.e. the interacting medium between the two aspects of duality.

The Number 2

From the number three we are further reduced to the number two, symbolizing duality. In Kemetic philosophy this number is referred to as the "two things that came into being in this land". The number one relates to non-duality. In Kemetic philosophy this number is related to the "first time" or beginning of Creation and referred to as the era "before two things had come into being in this land". Duality relates to the opposites of Creation (up-down, here-there, male-female, etc).

One and Ten

$$1 \Rightarrow \quad \text{Creation} \quad \Leftarrow 10$$

The number One is genderless and transcendental. In essence, all numbers are emanations from the number One. They are reflections of One in time and space, but the reflection is modified and conditioned. The Divine Whole Numbers are the clearest reflection of the basic principles in creation. The numbers 100 and 1000 and 1000000 are related to the number 10 and 10 to 1. Therefore, all Creation and its infinite manifestations and vast quantities as well as its vast fractions can be studied through the numbers from One to Ten.

$$(\infty)$$
$$\Downarrow$$
$$(1)$$
$$\Downarrow$$
$$(2) \Leftrightarrow (3)$$
$$\Downarrow$$
$$(4) \Leftrightarrow (5)$$
$$\Downarrow$$
$$(6) \Leftrightarrow (7)$$
$$\Downarrow$$
$$(8) \Leftrightarrow (9)$$
$$\Downarrow$$
$$(10)$$

The numbers One and Ten have a special relationship. Actually they are reflections of each other. Ten is the reflection of One. Therefore, the Bible says "human beings are made in God's image." With the understanding of Kemetic Philosophy, the higher truth within Christian religion becomes manifest. Heru is the Kemetic prototype for Christ in Christianity. He symbolizes perfection in life which is reached by living a life of truth and righteousness, i.e. upholding Maat. In the Temple of Heru in Egypt (city of Edfu) the Sanctuary (Holy of Holies) is encircled by a corridor and ten chapels. In the same temple Heru there are reliefs in which Heru can be seen harpooning Set ten times. Set (8) is the principle of egoism and unrighteousness in the human personality which must be subdued and sublimated in order to attain higher consciousness, i.e. to discover the mysteries of the other numbers and thereby attain spiritual enlightenment discovering the Supreme Being as the support and essence of Creation. Ten is the number of completeness since one cannot count beyond it without combining other numbers. However, the number one is undivided and all-encompassing. It is thus absolute and infinite. Therefore, Creation exists between One and Ten. As the characters of the Pautti are in reality aspects of human consciousness, the highest goal of all human beings is to attain the number Ten, i.e. to become Heru or in other terms, to attain Horushood and thereby reflect fully the glory of the Divine within themselves. Thus, the number one symbolizes the transcendent, i.e. the absolute, and the number ten symbolizes perfection in the world of time and space. Thus, the task of every human being is to discover their absolute and transcendental nature, Ra, and to become masters of their lives like Heru. In other words, the destiny of every human being is to discover their spirit nature and thus allow that nature to rule over the lower self, the ego, ignorance and vices.

ATUM AND THE MYSTERIES OF ANU

⌒

𓏲𓈖 *Atum (Tem)*

The sun and the moon were incorporated into the Ancient Egyptian worship from the most ancient times. The moon was symbolically associated with Asar, Aset and Djehuti, while the sun was symbolically associated with Ra, Ptah and Amun. According to the ancient creation story, the Supreme Being took the form of the sun god and arose out of the Primeval Ocean. According to one version, Ra arose in His boat along with the Ennead of gods and goddesses. According to another story, the Supreme Being arose in the form of a primeval hill or piece of solid land in the form of Atum, Tum or Tem. Thus, the Supreme Being who manifests as the rising sun out of the Primeval Ocean is known by various names. These are: Atum, Tum or Tem, Ra-Tem, Atum-Ra or Asar and Ptah. Atum is also one of the first god symbols to be depicted in human form. The priesthood of Anu developed an elaborate cosmology incorporating the concept of Tem into the creation myth, thereby merging human existence with the Divine. First we will review an outline of the theology of Anu, and then we will examine the mystical implications for human psycho-spirituality.

The *Pyramid Texts* of *Pepi II* determines the Company of Gods and Goddesses of Anu to be: Tem, Shu, Tefnut, Geb, Nut, Asar, Aset, Set and Nebethet. In the *Pyramid Texts* of *Pepi II,* the following account is given about the emergence of Atum (or Tem, Tum):

> He who was born in the Nu (primeval waters),
> before the sky came into being,
> before the earth came into being,
> before the two supports* came into being,
> before the quarrel** took place,
> before that fear which arose on account of the Eye of Heru existed...
>   *(Shu-Tefnut)
> **(quarrel between Heru and Set)

The idea of the Primeval Ocean (Nu) and the original primeval spirit which engendered life in it occurs in several myths. The earliest occurrence of the idea of the primeval waters is found in the Egyptian religion which predates the Asarian Resurrection Myth. This pre-dynastic (10,000-5,500 B.C.E.), pre-Asarian, myth spoke of a God who was unborn and undying, and who was the origin of all things. This deity was un-namable, unfathomable, transcendental, gender-less and without form, although encompassing all forms. This being was the God of Light which illumines all things, and thus was later associated with the sun, the forms of *Ra* or *Tem,* and with *Heru* who represents *that which is up there,* i.e., the Divine spirit. This form of Heru is the ancient one which predates the form of Heru sa Asar Aset (Heru the son of Osiris and Isis). The hieroglyphic spelling for the ancient form is:

𓊽 𓏙 𓅿 𓅆

Tum, Tem or Temu is an Ancient Egyptian name for the deep and boundless abyss of consciousness from which the phenomenal universe was born. *Khepera (or Khepri),* the dung beetle, represents the morning sun which is becoming. This form is also associated with the young Heru, *Heru in the Horizon,* also known as *The Sphinx.* Ra ☉ represents the daytime sun which sustains Creation. Tum comes from the root *tem* , "to be complete," "fullness" or *temem* , which means "to make an end of." Also Tum is regarded as the evening or setting sun in the western sky, symbolizing the completion, the end of the journey. This is why the initiate wishes to go to the *beautiful west* upon completion of the span of life. The beautiful west is the abode of Asar. Tum was analogous in nature to the Babylonian *Tiamat,* the Chaldean *Thamte,* the Hebrew *Tehorn,* and the Greek *Themis.*

Sundisk (Symbol of Ra)

The story related in the Papyrus of Nesi-Amsu is that the primeval God laid an egg in the primeval chaotic waters from which the God {him/her}self emerged. While this primordial God, who emerged out of the waters, created or emanated Ra, the Sun or Life Force, Djehuti, the word or creative medium, and Maat, the principle of cosmic order and regularity, the underlying emphasis was on all of these, as well as human beings and the phenomenal world, being essentially emanations from that same Primeval Ocean. Other stories tell of how the creator masturbated and engendered life through and within *Himself.* The papyrus of Nesi-Amsu further discusses the emergence:

> "When Atum emerged from Nun, the primordial waters, before the sky and earth were born and before the creation of worm or reptile, he found no place to stand..."

Tum, therefore represents the first emerging thought which contemplated its own existence in the vast ocean of undifferentiated consciousness which was devoid of names and forms, devoid of tangibleness, solidification, coagulation and grossness. All that existed was subtle matter, the Primeval Ocean. The *Pyramid Texts* continue, explaining how Atum continued the process of creation by emitting the other principles of creation in the form of the gods and goddesses as follows.

> "Tum (Atum) is he who came into being (through Himself) in Anu.
> He took His phallus in His grasp that he might create joy in Himself, emitting the twins Shu (air, dryness, space, ether) and Tefnut (moistness)..."

In this manner, the various qualities of matter emanated from Tum and gave form to the Primeval Ocean, and continue to give and sustain its form at every moment. Geb is the son of Shu and Tefnut and represents the solid earth. Nut is the daughter of Shu and Tefnut and represents the sky and the heavens, and is the mother of Asar, Aset, Set and Nebethet.

In a creation story involving Khepera (Ra in the aspect of the rising sun, the creation of a new day), he says he rose up from Nu and:

> "I found no place there whereon I could stand. I worked a charm upon my heart, I laid a foundation in Maa, and then I made every form. I was one by myself, {since} I had not yet emitted from myself the god Shu, and I had not spit out from myself the goddess Tefnut; there was no other being who worked with me."

PT 1248

"Atum begat creation by copulating with his hand."

His hand is his female nature and the priestess is the "wife" of the god, who facilitates the gods act of creation by performing the temple rituals and attending on the shrine of the divinity. – This format is the same in Amun system.

PT 1695

"Do not be far removed from the gods, I so th they may make for you this utterance which they made for Ra-Atum who shines every day. They will install you upon their thrones at the head of all the Ennead(s) as Ra and as his representative. They will bring you into being like Ra in this his name of Khepra; you will draw near to them like Ra in this his name of Ra; you will turn aside from their faces like Ra in this his name of Atum."

The passage above is the progenitor for the teachings in the Myth of Ra and Aset, presented below. They establish the nature of Ra-Atum and manifesting in the form of the solar Trinity.

Further, the Coffin Texts explain that Ra-Atum (or Atum-Ra) is none other than Ra and Asar merged into one.

Picture 15: Atum-Ra being attended on by the goddesses Aset and Nebethet

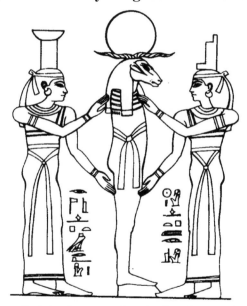

"This (Atum-Ra) is Asar resting in Ra, Ra resting in Asar."

Above: Another example of the Kemetic Caduceus, with Atum-Ra, symbolizing the central shaft, attended on by goddesses Nebethet and Aset.

After the millions of years of differentiated creation, the chaos that existed before creation will return; only the primeval god and Asar will remain steadfast-no longer separated in space and time.

—Ancient Egyptian Coffin Texts

The passage above concisely expresses the powerful teaching that all creation is perishable and that even the gods and goddesses will ultimately dissolve into the primordial state of potential consciousness. Therefore, it behooves a human being to move towards the Divine since that is the only stable truth that exists as an abiding reality. This is known as the Absolute, from which all has emanated and into which all will dissolve. *Tm* (Tem, Tum, Atum, Atum-Ra) is the Absolute, from which Creation arises and into which Creation will dissolve. A righteous person has the choice to go to the Djed and abide in Asar, to merge with him, or they can await the time when Ra traverses through the Duat, the eternal journey described earlier, illuminating it as He passes in his Boat. If they choose Ra, they will be picked up and be loaded unto the boat where they will merge with Ra and experience peace, bliss and happiness for all time. The *Book of Amduat* discusses the Duat with the followers of Ra in mind, while the *Prt m Hru* and the *Book of Gates* discusses the Duat with the followers of Asar in mind. If they choose to stay in the Duat, they will lead a life in the astral plane similar to that on earth for a certain period of time but with very important differences. These differences are outlined in Chapter 8 of the Ancient Egyptian *Book of Coming Forth By Day*. The same transcendental and non-dualist philosophy evident in the passage above from the *Coffin Texts* can be found in the Indian *Upanishads*.

> *Before creation came into existence, Brahman (the Absolute) existed as the Unmanifest. From the Unmanifest was created the manifest. From himself he brought forth himself. Hence he is known as the Self-Existent.*
>
> —Taittiriya Upanishad

The Ancient Egyptian concept of Nun is powerfully expressed in the following passage from the *Coffin Texts.*

> *I am Nu, The Only One, without equal and I came into being at the time of my flood...I originated in the primeval void. I brought my body into existence through my own potency. I made myself and formed myself in accordance with my own desire. That which emanated from me was under my control.*

Once again, the initiate is to discover that the Divine Self is the substratum of manifest creation and that {his/her} deeper essence and the deeper essence of all humanity is that same Self-existent Divinity which brought the entire creation into being by the power of her own will and desire. Nun is an aspect of Tem. In this aspect, it is to be understood as a formless potential matter which can convert itself into any form and any element (earth, water, fire, metal, etc.). This process may be likened to how temperature affects water. For example, very cold water becomes ice, and ice can have any shape. When very hot, the water evaporates and becomes so subtle (vapor) as to be "unmanifest." At room temperature, he same water is visible but formless. All matter is like the water. All matter is composed of the same essence which takes on the form of various objects, just as clay can take many forms. However, the forms are not abiding but temporary. God has assumed the forms of Creation just as an actor assumes a part in a play. When the play is over, the actor's mask is stripped away and the true essence of the actor's identity is revealed, just as ice melts to reveal water. The Divine Self is the substratum of all that is manifest. The same philosophy, and using almost the same exact language, is evident in the Indian *Upanishads.*

> *...In the beginning there was Existence alone—One only, without a second. He, the One, thought to himself: Let me be many, let me grow forth. Thus, out of himself he projected the universe; and having projected the universe out of himself the universe he entered into every being.*
>
> —Chandogya Upanishad

Ultimately though, in reality there is only one abode for the soul, and that is, the Divine Self, which transcends even Tem, that being from which rises Ra, Asar and all Creation. This is confirmed in all versions of the *Prt m Hru* and is perhaps most succinctly expressed in the *Coffin Texts,* where it is explained that there is an even more subtle essence beyond Atum, that is unknown by men, and nameless. The initiate, reading the following passages, is to make the following realizations.

I am the Double Lion (i.e. eternal), older than Atum.

I am Ra, who is exalted forever, I am Atum, more of a spirit (i.e. subtler) *than the other spirits.*
I am the Lord of Eternity.

I am the Only One, who journeys over the Primeval Void.
I am the One whose name is not known by human beings.

This means that essentially, Asar and Ra are actually one being. This is most clearly demonstrated by the depiction of Asar, in a Divine Boat (Neshmet). This is one reason why the moon was chosen as a symbol of Asar. It is said that Ra has the Moon and Sun as his eyes, and either works as a passageway to the deeper transcendental Self, just as the eyes of a human being act as a window into the inner Self. This idea of the oneness of the Supreme Being is stated again directly in the image above which reads: *This is Asar resting in Ra, Ra resting in Asar.* The two great goddesses Nebethet and Aset attend on Atum Ra as he stands on the pedestal of Maat. Once again, the image of the Trinity is given with one male aspect and two females aspects, symbolizing non-duality (one God, one Spirit) and duality (two goddesses), respectively. The concept of two paths is evident in the very decision to present the culmination of the spiritual journey in the form of two chapters wherein the spiritual aspirant can join Ra (Chapter 35) or Asar (Chapter 36). This presentation points to the highly advanced philosophical view that the Ancient Egyptian Sages were putting forth, that the gods and goddesses (Neteru) are merely images for worship, and are not to be seen as ultimate or absolute realities in and of themselves. They are to be understood as windows into the transcendent, avenues by which the energies of the mind and body may be channeled towards a higher, spiritual goal in life. Not until Vedanta philosophy emerges in India, is there another form of mysticism like it in the world.

On Following page: King Kafra, protected and enlivened by Ra in the form of Heru, the Solar Hawk

ANUNIAN THEOLOGY: THE MYSTICAL PHILOSOPHY OF RA RELIGION

Study of the Ancient Egyptian Hieroglyph "Ben" and tracing its mystical teaching through Anunian Theology

The Ancient Egyptian term Ben is the basis for a deep philosophy related to the emergence of Creation and serves as the key to unlock the formulas contained in its derivative terms as well as the mystical symbolism of the architecture and symbols present in Anu, the city of Ra, and in Menefer, the place of the beautiful monuments (pyramids and sphinx of Giza.

A. The Kemetic (Ancient Egyptian) solar principle is based on the most ancient concept of Heru. The hieroglyphic spelling of the term provides insight into the nature of the philosophical teaching.

Heru - Ancient name spelled out

Herut - female form of ancient Heru

The determinative symbol is the first important key in understanding the concept of Heru. It means person or entity. The next important symbols are the hawk and god-divinity. The other symbols are phonetic or determinative, denoting the sound of the words and their gender. The concept of Heru denotes the spirit, which is on high and all-encompassing and existing in the male as well as the female form. These forms were later developed into the divinities Heru sa Asar Aset (Horus son of Osiris and Isis) for the male aspect and Het Heru (House of Horus) for the female aspect.

B. Heru is spirit but manifests through the first principle that emerges in the primeval ocean, i.e. Atum. Atum emerges from the primeval water and establishes the first "solid" place or ***ben*** and from here the phenomenal "solid" world is created.

benu – sacred stone which the divinity of light first created as the first solid matter from the primeval ocean. Also, it is the capstone on the pyramid and obelisks.

C. The Ben stone was used to create the ***Benben*** monuments, the body of the pyramid and obelisks.

BenuBenu stone - obelisk – pyramid

Benben also relates to fire offerings and light from the sun.

Ben Ben - fire offering in house of Seker

Ben Ben - god of light in temple of Seker

Benben also relates to the sacred solar bird of Ra who *burns* up periodically but emerges from the ashes, renewed and radiant.

benu bird – phoenix – Solar bird of Ra

D. This concept of the benben has been adopted symbolically by the United States of America as an attempt to associate the socio-political ideas of that country with the spiritual-philosophical concepts of Ancient Egypt by its use as the seal of the United States of America, commonly found on its currency. Also, the concept of Techenu, the obelisk, from Ancient Egypt as also been adopted symbolically only, as the United States of America associates neither with the religion of ancient Egypt or its social philosophy, but rather with its great achievement as the first civilization in history.

Picture 16: Left- Example of a Benben (capstone) also referred to as pyramidon stone- made for Psammentichus II. Right- Pyramid seal of the United States of America.

E. The most sacred benbens were kept in the cities of Anu and Hetkaptah (Heliopolis and Memphis) and their attendant burial/ritual transformation grounds (Giza and Sakkara respectively).

Het ben ben m Anu - Shrine of the benben stone in city of Ra.

het benben - house of the benben in pyramid district (Giza).

Men nefer –Place (district) of the beautiful pyramid- Memphis, Sakkara, Giza, Abusir, Meidum and the other cites of the major pyramid complexes.

According to the Sarcophagus of Seti I, the Duat is the body of the god Asar, which is pictured as a man bending backwards into a circle, touching his toes with his hands. It is said to have fourteen *Aats* or regions. The ultimate destination of all departed souls is the region of the Duat called *Sekhet Yaru.* Sekhet Yaru means "Field of Plants." It is located within the region called *Sekhet Hetep* or "Field of Peace." Hetep may be translated as peace and/or offerings which make peace. Thus, the pyramid district is to be understood as the doorway to the region in which the astral plane is accessed. In this capacity it must be understood that there is a difference between monument or ritual pyramids, which are temples, as opposed to burial pyramids which serve the purpose of holding the body within the Mer or primeval mound (or mountain), i.e. the pyramid (ex. Pyramid of Unas and other small burial pyramid tombs).

Mer - pyramid

or **Aa - pyramid tomb glyphs**

Aat - pyramid region - cemetary-other world glyph.

THE TANTRIC SYMBOLISM OF THE ANCIENT EGYPTIAN PYRAMID

The Ancient Egyptian Pyramid represents important tantric symbolism. It provides mystical insight into the nature of numbers and to the relationship between the physical world and the transcendental Self. The mystical symbolism of the number four refers to the four sides of the pyramid (d-e-f-g).

Picture 17: The Pyramid when viewed from directly overhead

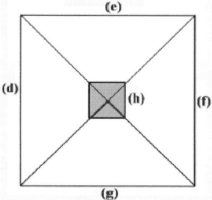

Four is the number of time and space, the physical universe. The single side of the pyramid, being a triangle, represents the number three as well as the Trinity of existence which manifests both as a Divine Trinity of Gods and Goddesses in the form of Father, Mother and Child such as

Osiris, Isis and Horus or the Divine Trinity of Amun, Ra, Ptah, who refer to the triad of human consciousness (waking, dream and deep sleep) and the essence of existence (witnessing consciousness, mind and the physical universe (see the book *The Hymns of Amun* by Dr. Muata Ashby. The number four is an emanation of the number three and the number three is an emanation of the number two and the number two (duality) is an emanation of the one, singular and non-dual essence (God). Thus, the multiplicity comes together at the top (h) into one point, known as the *Eye of Horus* which represents universal consciousness. Thus, the pyramid is a Tantric symbol which shows how creation and the Divine are inseparably related.

Picture 18: The Pyramid when viewed from the side, showing the Eye of Heru capstone.

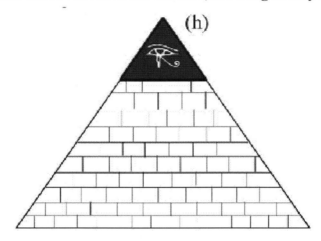

The Forms of Atum: From Heru to Heru m Akhet

The deeper meaning of the divinity Atum may be discovered by examining the descriptions and associations given in the Pyramid Texts and Books of the Dead as well as other related papyri related to Atum and Anunian Theology. The hieroglyphic texts describing the forms of the solar divinity contain significant keys to understanding the mysteries of the solar religious practice and its attendant mystical teachings.

Atm or Tm, (Tem, Tum, Atum, Atum-Ra), is the ultimate source and cause of Creation. From Tm arises Khepri who transforms into Ra and finally, Ra reverts back to the original essence, Tm.

Atum is related to Amun, Ra and Khepra:

Amun- Hidden essential nature, i.e. underlying consciousness.
Ra – The term Ra is associated with *Akhu* the shining spirit – light.

> *Tum-Khepera* – The Creator
> *Ra-Tum* – Sustainer
> *Amun-Ra-Tum* – The hidden essence manifesting as the sustaining and completing divinity.

Atum is related to Heru

Heru- The Supreme Light

Herakhti – at least three spellings are given for this term and they mean:

"*Heru of the two horizons*" [hieroglyphs] or [hieroglyphs] or

"*Heru of the two spirit lands*" [hieroglyphs] or

"*Heru of the two abodes*" [hieroglyphs],

From these spellings the idea emerges of Ra-Herakhti [hieroglyphs] as the manifestation of the spirit in a dual form, i.e. the physical realm and the spirit realm. This concept becomes clearer when the term Ra-Herakhti, Rwti and Her m Akht are seen as referring to the same divinity.

Atum is related to the Sphinx, which is called *Hu* in Ancient Egyptian.

[hieroglyphs] *Hu* - sphinx

The Solar divinity (Atum, Ra) is referred to as: "*Heru khuti Tem, The Lord of the Two Lands of Anu*" and "*The Dweller in Behdet,*" i.e. Heru.

Herukhuti–Ra-Tem-Khepera – Pharaoh Djehutimes IIII refers to the Great Sphinx at Giza by this term. Therefore, the Sphinx is regarded as a form of Herukhuti or Herakhti.

Heru-m-akht- Sphinx - Heru manifesting in the horizon.

Ra-Herakhti - The Pharaoh Djehutimes (Thutmosis) dug out and repaired the great sphinx, which was in disrepair and being covered by desert sands, and reestablished worship of *Ra-Herakhti.*

From the 75 Praises of Ra- (from the tombs of the XIXth and XX dynasties at Waset (Thebes).

"Ra is the Double Sphinx God"

Atum is the Double Lion God

In the Pyramid Texts it is related that the initiate (king) experiences the fate as the Double Lion God.

PT 696

If the King be hungry, the [hieroglyphs] *Rwti* (Double Lion-god) will be hungry…

Rwti means: double lion - Ra Herakhti or Shu and Tefnut or two of the gods who act as judges for Asar. Further, it is explained that the Double Lion God is Atum. Therefore, the initiate is "rise" up to and become one with Atum, the sun, i.e. the spirit, for the sun is the manifestation of the divinity and not the divinity itself.

PT 2081-2082

Lift up this King's double to the god, lead him to the *Rwti* (Double Lion-god), cause him to mount up to Atum, for Atum has done what he said he would do for this King…

The Term *Rwti* and *Herakhti*

Rwti means double lions. It refers to Atum manifesting in dual form as Shu and Tefnut (space-air and consciousness-water). The terms *Rwti* and *Herakhti* appear to hold the same meaning and are used interchangeably as a reference for the concept of Heru manifesting on the two horizons (dawn and sunset) i.e. encompassing the beginning and the end of things.

The Term *Her m Akht*

The term *Her m Akht* does not appear in Ancient Egypt until the New Kingdom Period. However, it appears to be a new term given to the Sphinx, which was previously called Herukhuti or Herakhti since the Pyramid Text period.

Thus, Atum, Ra, Heru, Rwti, Hu, and Herukhuti are all relating to the same divinity. In mystical terms they relate to the divine spirit, Ra, who is Supreme, Heru, and yet manifesting as the master of the world in the form of the Great Sphinx in Giza, Egypt, and also the Great Sphinx in the heavens as the constellation Leo.

The term **Herakhti** 𓅃 𓈌 𓈌, may be understood as Heru, the double horizon and the term **Herumakht** 𓅃 𓄿 𓈌, may be understood as Heru manifesting in the horizon. The sun in between the two mountains of the valley (Akher-the two lions of Yesterday and Tommorow) represents the eternal spirit traversing in between the duality, the temporal.

Shu and Tefnut are also known as the Akheru (leonine) divinities. That is, they are the lion and lioness who guard the Akhet (horizon) which is entrance to the Netherworld, i.e. they are the boundary between the Netherworld and the Physical World, depending on which perspective is used. The lions are symbolic of the mountains flanking the valley through which the dead souls and the dieing sun must pass.

Picture 19: Akhet, the horizon, with the sundisk.

From the point of view of creation, they are the first physical entities created by Ra and are thus the passageway of the spirit into the realm or plane of matter, time and space. This is why they are associated with the Akheru, who represent yesterday and tomorrow, i.e. the principle of duality.

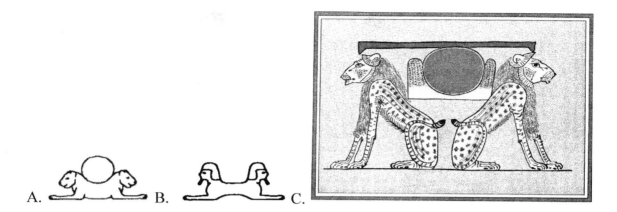

Plate 1: A-Akheru, the lion gods of Yesterday and Tomorrow with Sundisk. B. With human heads. C. Akher and Akhet together as one.

The sun traverses between the Akheru, i.e. the past and the future. Therefore, always remaining in the eternal present. This is deeper mystical teaching for every spiritual aspirant to understand, how not to get caught up in the pettiness of life and the tension, and anxiety over what happened in the past and the tension, and anxiety over what is desired in the future. In *Pyramid Texts* 796, 1014 and 1713 it is stated of the righteous soul: *the gates of Akher are opened for you.* The eternal present is the pathway between the physical plane and the astral plane. The past and the future do not exist. Only eternity is real.

Herakhti as the Her-m-akht: The Sphinx

Another related term to *Herakhti* 𓃀𓏤𓏤, which may be understood as Heru, the double horizon and the term *Hermakht* 𓃀 𓃀 𓏤, which may be understood as Heru manifesting in the horizon (both explained earlier, is the term *Hu n Heru m Akht.* The sun in, *Hu n Heru m Akht,* literally means "The sphinx of Heru who manifests in the horizon." Therefore, we are to understand that the sphinx in Egypt, located in Giza, has a counterpart in the horizon. This concept may be seen in two ways.

𓀭𓂝𓂻𓃀𓏤𓈖𓉐𓊖 **or** 𓀭𓃀𓂻𓈖𓃀𓏤

Hu m menu nefer or hu m n herakhti -sphinx of the district with the pyramid monuments (i.e. the Giza plateau)

𓃀𓏤 or 𓃀𓏤 Herakhti

𓃀𓏤𓃀𓏤 Herakhuti

The Anunian Goddesses Aspect of the Supreme Being in the form of the God Atum

Anunian theology ascribes three forms of the solar creative principle with female aspects. These are Heru, Ra and Atum, who are aspects of each other. Therefore, their female counterparts are also aspects of each other as well. The female aspect of Heru, Hetheru and the female aspect of Ra, Rat, were discussed earlier. Here we will briefly discuss the nature of the goddess principle related to Atum.

Atum has not one but two female divinities associated with him. Much like Asar, and his relationship to Aset and Nebthet, these two goddesses symbolize the dynamic aspect of the divinity in his two major forms of manifestation.

Picture 20: Goddess Iusaasety-Nebthotep

The goddess principle of Atum is actually a two aspected divinity herself. One form is called Iusaasety which means goddess of movement. The other is called Nebthotep which means Mistress of Offerings and Peace. Therefore, it is obvious that this symbolism is relating the dual qualities of Ra which manifest through the goddess aspect. These qualities are Movement on one end and inertia (inertness) on the other. Through the interaction of these two principles, the Supreme Divinity, in the form of Atum, carries out the work of Creation. Therefore, we have another Trinity in Anunian Theology which is composed of Spirit, movement and inertia. Embedded in the hieroglyphic spelling of the names of these goddesses can be found the seed of the names for the goddesses Aset and Nebethet. Further, the two aspected goddess nature represents the important principle of the opposites of Creation.

Atum

Iusaasety ⇔ Nebthotep

The History of Manetho

The evidence concerning the new dating of the sphinx affects the treatment of the History of Manetho. Manetho was one of the last Ancient Egyptian High Priests who retained the knowledge of the ancient history of Egypt. In 241 B.C.E. he was commissioned to compile a series of wisdom texts by King Ptolemy II, one of the Macedonian (Greek) rulers of Egypt after it was captured and controlled by the Greeks. One of Manetho's compositions included a history of Egypt. However, Manetho's original writings did not survive into the present. Therefore, the accounts of his writings by the Greeks who studied his work constitute the current remaining record of his work, and some of the accounts differ from each other in certain respects. His history has come down to us in the form of translation, part of which are missing certain portions. However, it has been ascertained that he grouped the Dynastic Rulers of Ancient Egypt into 30 Dynasties containing around 330 Pharaohs in a period of around 4,500 years (going back from his time-241 B.C.E.). According to Manetho Ancient Egyptian chronology included the following periods:

1- **The Gods** - This period was the genesis. It began with the emergence of the great Ennead or Company of gods and goddesses headed by Ra, the Supreme Being. The God, Ra himself, ruled over the earth.

2- **The Demigods** - After the Gods, the Demigods ruled the earth. Then came a descendent line of royal rulers followed by 30 rulers in the city of Memphis. These were followed by another set of royal rulers. The Heru Shemsu often mentioned in various texts referring to the ancient worship of Heru as the Supreme Spirit belong to this age.

3- **The Spirits of the Dead** - After the period of the Demigods came the Spirits of the Dead.

According to the Turin Papyrus (original Ancient Egyptian document dating to c 1440 B.C.E.), the dates of the periods are:

1- **The Gods** – 23,200

2- **The Demigods** – 13,420

3- **The Spirits of the Dead** – cannot be deciphered due to damage on the document.

Total: Total: 36,620 years before the unification.

According to Eusebius, the dates of the periods of Ancient Egypt **_before_** Menes, the uniter of the two lands into one empire, total: 28,927 years before the unification.

According to Diodorus of Sicily, the dates of the periods total 33,000 before the unification.

These periods were then followed by the Dynastic Period which is the only period of Ancient Egypt of which most people have knowledge (c. 5,000 B.C.E.-30 B.C.E.). Due to the deficiencies in the historical record an exact dating for each period preceding the dynastic is not available. However, it is reasonably certain that the total number of years outlined above goes back in history to at least 28,927 years from the time when Manetho was writing in 241 B.C.E. This gives a total of number of years around the beginning of the preceding "Great Year" preceding the current one.

4- Mortal Human Beings – i.e. The Pre-Dynastic and Dynastic Periods-
Rulership by Pharaohs (Kings and Queens).

This period must be divided into the Pre-Dynastic age and the Dynastic age, for the Dynastic age that is often used to represent the beginning of Ancient Egyptian civilization only refers to the time of the major unification of all the kingdoms (nomes) of the Southern ands Northern portions of the country into one single nation.

The Pharaonic (royal) calendar based on the Sothic system (star Sirius) containing cycles of 1,460 years, was in use by 4,241 B.C.E. This certainly required extensive astronomical skills and time for observation. The Sothic system is based on the *Heliacal* (i.e. appears in the sky just as the sun breaks through the eastern horizon) rising of the star Sirius in the eastern sky, signaling the new year as well as the inundation season. Therefore, the history of Kamit (Egypt) must be reckoned to be extremely ancient. Thus, in order to grasp the antiquity of Ancient Egyptian culture, religion and philosophy, we will review the calendar systems used by the Ancient Egyptians.

The calendar based on the Great Year was also used by the Ancient Egyptians. The Great year is founded on the movement of the earth through the constellations known as the *Precession of the Equinoxes.* It is confirmed by the history given by the Ancient Egyptian Priest Manetho in the year 241 B.C.E. Each Great Year has 25,860 to 25,920 years and 12 arcs or constellations, and each passage through a constellation takes 2,155 – 2,160 years. These are the "Great Months" of the "Great Year." The current cycle or year began at around 10,858 B.C.E. At about the year 36,766 B.C.E., according to Manetho, the Creator, Ra, ruled the earth in person from his throne in the Ancient Egyptian city of Anu (Greek-Heliopolis-city of the sun). By this reckoning our current year (2,000 A.C.E.) is actually the year 38,766 based on the Great Year System of Ancient Egyptian reckoning.

The period of 36,525 years is also 25 times 1,460 which is the cycle of the helical rising of Sirius. The Sirian calendar was another time reckoning system based on the star Sirius and its relation with the sun of our solar system which contains a cycle of 1,460 years. An inscription by Censorinus in forms us that the rising of Sirius occurred in 139 A.C.E. This means that the Sirian cycle also occurred in the years 1321 B.C.E, 2781 B.C.E, and 4241 B.C.E. By means of two inscriptions from the 18th Dynasty it has been reliably established that the date for the 18th Dynasty is 1580 B.C.E. The first verifiable use of the calendar occurs in the year 4241 B.C.E. The calendar based on the Great Year was also used by the Ancient Egyptians. The Great year is based on the astronomical movement of the earth through the constellations known as the precession of the Equinoxes. It is confirmed by the history given by the Ancient Egyptian Priest Manetho in the year 241 B.C.E. Each Great Year has 25,860 to 25,920 years and 12 arcs or constellations, and each passage through a constellation takes 2,155 – 2,160 years. These are the "Great Months." The current cycle or year began around the year 10858 B.C.E. According to the reckoning based on Manetho's history, if we take the average number of years in the Great Year and add it to the known year of the beginning of the current year we get a total of 36,748 (25,890 + 10,858=36,748). If we compare this number with the history of Manetho we find a difference of 18 years, accountable by the deterioration in the translated records and the variance in the number of years in the Great Year cycle. Thus, we have match that supports the History and the practice of reckoning time by the Great Year. So we have reliable confirmations that the Sirian calendar was in use in Ancient Egypt at least as early as 4241 B.C.E. and that a greater form of reckoning, the Great Year, corroborates the History of Manetho which takes Ancient Egyptian chronology and civilized use of mathematics, astronomy and time reckoning back to 36,748 B.C.E. This longer duration cycle system of time reckoning was supported by recent discoveries.

That the Egyptians handled astronomical cycles of even greater duration is indicated by inscriptions recently found by Soviet archeologists in newly opened graves during the period of their work on the Aswan Dam. Here the cycles appear to cover periods of 35,525 years, which would be the equivalent of 25 cycles of 1461 years. The apparent discrepancy of one year in this recording of cycles is due to the sothic cycle of 1460 years being the equivalent of a civil cycle of 1461 years. According to Muck there were three main cycles: one of 365 X 4 = 1460; another of 1460 X -25 = 36,500; and a third of 36,500 X 5 = 182,500 years.

It has been proposed as a support of the use of the Great Year calendar that the Ancient Egyptians instituted the use of different symbolisms in religion and government in accordance with the current symbolism of the particular age in question. Thus, during the age (great month) of Leo, the lion symbolism would be used. What is compelling about this rationale is that the new evidence in reference to the age of the Sphinx coincides with the commencement of the New Great Year and the age of Leo, which began in 10,858 B.C.E. However, when it is understood that the damage on the sphinx would have required thousands of years to produce and when the history of Manetho as well as the conjunction of the Sphinx with the constellation Leo when it makes its heliacal rising at the beginning of each Great Year, it becomes possible to envision the possibility that the Sphinx was created at the beginning of the previous Great Year anniversary (36,748 B.C.E.). The Great sphinx and its attendant monuments as well as other structures throughout Egypt which appear to be compatible architecturally should therefore be considered as part of a pinnacle of high culture that was reached well before the dynastic age, i.e. previous to 5,000 B.C.E. The form of the Sphinx itself, displaying the lion body with the human head but also with the particularly "leonine" headdress including the lion's mane, was adopted by the Pharaohs of the Dynastic Period. In the Ancient Egyptian mythological system of government, the Pharaoh is considered as a living manifestation of Heru and he or she wields the leonine power which comes from the sun, Ra, in order to rule. The sundisk is the conduit through which the Spirit transmits Life Force energy to the world, i.e. the Lion Power, and this force is accessed by turning towards the Divine in the form of the sun. Hence, the orientation of the Sphinx towards the east, facing the rising sun. All of this mystical philosophy and more is contained in the symbolic-metaphorical form and teaching of the Sphinx. Thus, we have a link of Ancient Egyptian culture back to the Age of Leo and the commencement of the current cycle of the Great Year in remote antiquity. Other ages and symbolisms of the zodiac that have been identified include the Ram, and the bull.

Picture 21: Above- The Hor-m-akhet (Sphinx) Pharaonic headdress.

Picture 22: Below- Modern renditions of the Sphinx showing the prominent leonine headdress.

Picture 23: The Great Heru m Akhet (Sphinx) of Ancient Egypt.

The Sphinx is the oldest known monument and it relates to the solar mysticism of Anu as well as to the oldest form of spiritual practice known. From it we also derive certain important knowledge in reference to the antiquity of civilization in Ancient Egypt.

Picture 24: Constellation Leo-The Lion

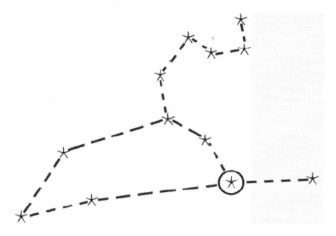

The Great Sphinx faces due east and in the year c. 10,800 B.C.E. a perfect conjunction is created as the Sphinx faces the rising sun and the constellation Leo, the lion.

Picture 25: The Sphinx faces due east at the beginning of the Great year and faces the Constellation Leo as it makes its Heliacal Rising.

Picture 26: The Great Heru m akhet (Sphinx) of Egypt.

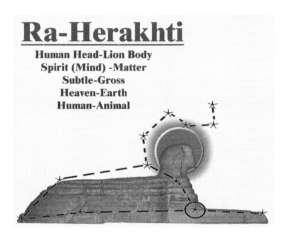

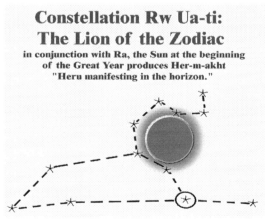

The Great Year is a system of time reckoning based on the precession of the equinoxes. Precession is the slow revolution of the Earth's axis of rotation (wobbling) about the poles of the ecliptic. It is caused by lunar and solar perturbations acting on the Earth's equatorial bulge and causes a westward motion of the stars that takes 25,800 years to complete. At the beginning of the Great Year, around 10,800-10,500 B.C.E. the constellation Leo rose up in the sky along the line of the ecliptic just as the sun dawned at the same time, marking the beginning of the current great year cycle which lasts 25,800 years.

The sphinx on earth as a counterpart to the sphinx in the heavens.

The sphinx on earth as a counterpart to the sphinx in the heavens (Astral Plane), i.e. the horizon of the earth plane and the horizon of the astral plane. In this view, the sphinx on earth and the sphinx in heaven complement each other and form two halves of the akher-akhet symbol but turned facing each other, looking at the sun which is between them, i.e. turning away from the earth plane and towards the transcendental spirit.

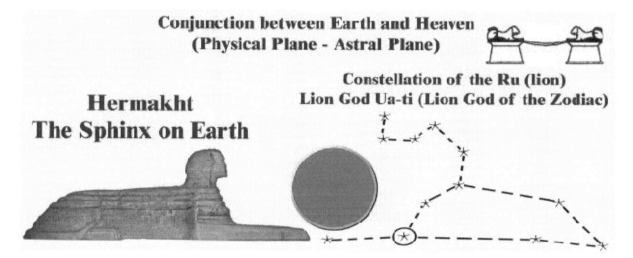

Conjunction between Earth and Heaven
(Physical Plane - Astral Plane)

Constellation of the Ru (lion)
Lion God Ua-ti (Lion God of the Zodiac)

Hermakht
The Sphinx on Earth

The Anunian Temple: Cosmic Symbolism in the Solar Temple Architecture

The Benben, Tekhenu and Mer Temples

The pyramids (**Mer**) and obelisks (**Tekhenu**) are actually symbols of the primeval stone of creation upon which the spirit, in the form of the sun, first shone at the time of Creation. This stone is a metaphor of all that is solid, congealed and tangible upon which human life is based. In this sacred places, reenactments of the Mysteries of Creation, that have been described in this volume, were carried out.

Picture 27: Basic Ancient Egyptian Pyramid Temple Complex

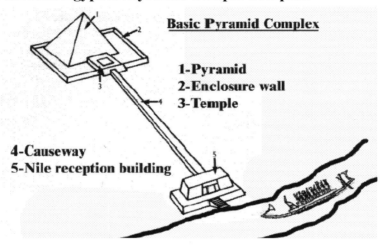

Picture 28: Basic Ancient Egyptian Obelisk Temple Complex

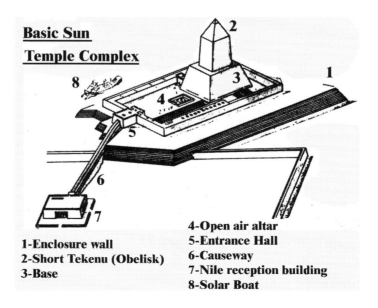

1-Enclosure wall
2-Short Tekenu (Obelisk)
3-Base

4-Open air altar
5-Entrance Hall
6-Causeway
7-Nile reception building
8-Solar Boat

Above: Step Pyramid of Sakkara

Geb and Nut and the Obelisk

The tantric teachings of Egypt are embodied in the creation stories which involve the emanation of the *neters* from *The Neter*. As soon as the pairs of neters (*Shu and Tefnut, Geb and Nut, Osiris and Isis, Horus and Hathor, Set and Nephthys, etc.*) arise out of the Supreme, Androgynous Being, there is a tantric relationship being described. The next teaching of Tantrism appear in the relationships between the neters which comprise the companies of the major theological systems.

Picture 29: Geb and Nut after separating from their sexual union.

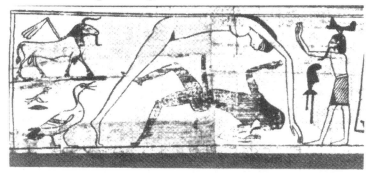

One of the most ancient creation myths of Egypt tells of how Ra (Supreme Being) emerged out of the primeval waters and from Ra emanated Geb and Nut in this cosmological system. Geb represents the earth or physical nature, and Nut represents the heavens or the subtle nature of creation. In the beginning creation consisted of Heaven and Earth and nothing else because they held each other in such a tight embrace that it did not allow anything to exist. So creation consisted of the separation of heaven and earth through the medium of space and time (Shu). Thus, Ra separated Geb and Nut with Shu or space-ether. There are many depictions of Geb and Nut after their separation by Shu. Geb is lying on his back or sitting on the ground and sometimes he is depicted with an erect penis, pointing up toward Nut, whom he has just been separated from.

One of the most important tantric symbols related to Geb and Nut is the Obelisk. The obelisk is a tall structure which tapers toward the top wherein there is a small pyramid structure. It may be inscribed with hieroglyphic writing. The obelisk is a symbol of the penis of Geb. It rises out of the earth and reaches up toward the sky, reminding us of the original separation which caused heaven and earth to come into being. The deeper mystical symbolism of the obelisk can be seen when it is viewed from a distance. The space around it symbolizes heaven. Therefore, heaven and earth, though appearing to be separate, are in reality always one if the earth itself is viewed from outer space it is surrounded and enfolded by the heavens. This is exactly what is being conveyed through the depiction of Nut enveloping Geb from east to west. This is the underlying oneness of creation and it is the same oneness which must be realized in the human heart. Though appearing to be separate from creation, in reality, every human being is enfolded by and indeed one with creation. Therefore, rituals developed wherein the symbolic raising of the obelisk were equated with the raising of the human soul to discovering its oneness with creation to be established (Tettu) in a vertical movement which is rooted in physical nature (Geb), while at the same time being in touch with the spirit (Nut). As long as there is separateness from creation, the feeling that one is a separate and finite individual, then there can be no true peace, contentment or happiness. The supreme Being and creation are one and the same. Also the Soul of every individual and the Supreme Being are one and the same. Therefore, uniting with the universe is the natural progression of self-discovery. The separation and individuality experienced by most people and reinforced by society is an expression of ignorance of the truth.

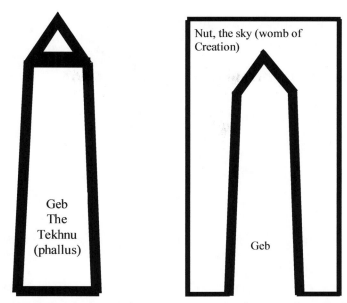

Above left: The Obelisk represents the penis of Geb (earth). The skyline around it is Nut (heavens-cosmos). Thus, by directing sexual energy toward heaven, the unification of heaven and earth within oneself may be effected.

Above right: Nut, that which surrounds and encompassed the Obelisk. Nut is everything adjacent to the Geb (earth) and therefore symbolizes the unity of creation. As a polar principle, Nut represents the female aspect of creation and Geb represents the male. However, the two together are seen as complementary symbolic elements of the original matrices, The Supreme Self.

According to the Creation Myth, The Supreme Being created the Goddess **NUT** (Sky-Heaven-Fire) and the God **GEB** (Earth-Solid). The God **GEB** and the Goddess **NUT** represent the male and female principles of creation, respectively. Then the Supreme "nameless" GOD created **SHU** (air) to separate heaven and earth, making a physical world and a heavenly world. Thus it is through the separation of Heaven and Earth by the god **SHU** that the universe was created.

The ***"Obelisk"***, a tall tapering tower with a pyramid at the top, represents the erectile power of the physical human body as personified by the god of the earth principle, Geb. Our physical nature, though susceptible to the temptations of the flesh, is capable of great energy. In viewing any Obelisk, it should be noted that it represents a phallus uniting "Heaven and Earth" as it reaches up out of the earth *(Geb)*, through the air *(Shu)*, towards Heaven *(Nut),* just as an erect phallus on a man's body projects up out and away from his body. As it projects it is unifying with space. Thus, symbolically, an obelisk represents the unity of the female and male powers (Heaven and Earth). A brief stud of the hieroglyphs of the obelisk reveals its mysticism.

Tekhnu means obelisk. This term is phonetically related to or or *tkh* or *tkhy* or *tkhu* which means vibrating plummet for the scales – vibration. Tkh is related to or *Tekhi* - ibis - ibis god of the judgment of the heart –Djehuti. *Tekhii* is also god of the first month –again Djehuti. Also it is related to tekhnu – to beat a drum – cause vibration - play music. Thus, tekhnu means, the place where the first vibration occurred which brought creation into being, i.e., the first utterance of God of his own name which caused ripples in the primeval ocean and caused the waters to turn into the forms of Creation.

Picture 30: Hoeing the Earth and Raising the Obelisk

The obelisk is related to the mysticism of resurrection. It is commensurate with the raising of the pillar of Asar in the Asarian Mysteries (recall that Asar is the first born son of Geb). In the Pyramid Texts 1394-5 it is said "The earth is hacked up by the hoe, the offering is presented ... 0 Geb, open your mouth for your son Asar." All human beings (male and female) become Asar at the time of their physical death. Book of the Dead contains the statement "I have received the hoe on the day of hacking up the earth." This statement is followed by the propitiation: "May you cause to enter the perfect soul ... into the house of Asar." Geb, being the god of the earth, receives the bodies of all human beings. Therefore it is important to "hoe" the earth by cultivating positive actions so that one may be worthy to pass through the physical nature and enter into the netherworld. This development is symbolized by the raising of the obelisk, which is tantamount to arousal of the sex energy and its sublimation into a transcendental movement upwards towards the sky, wherein waits Nut to receive the righteous souls. In the tomb of Rekhmira at Thebes the rite of hoeing the earth and raising the obelisk are depicted at the entrance to his tomb.

Picture 31: The Phenomenal Sphinx (left) meets the Cosmic Sphinx (right) in the form of the Constellation Leo The Lion

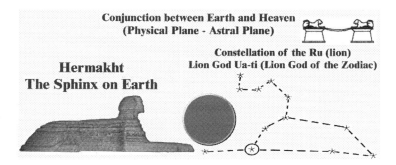

NOTE: For greater insight into this picture see the one above entitled *"The Sphinx faces due east at the beginning of the Great year and faces the Constellation Leo as it makes its Heliacal Rising"* which presents this same image but looking from the West. When viewed from the side (north or south) the image of the cosmic Akhet emerges.

Picture 32: Sphinx Glyphs used to symbolize the actual monuments created for the Sphinx causeways at various temples.

The New Kingdom Era temples actually continue the solar mysticism as they recreate the akhet symbol ⌂. Each pylon symbolizes the two lions, Akher, as well as the two sides of the valley through which the sun moves. This means that every initiate is like the sun, moving through duality and into eternity as the greater the movement, the closer the initiate moves towards the holy of holies wherein the deepest mysteries are discovered and all ignorant mortal existence comes to an end just as the setting sun brings forth the end of the day, the end of Creation.

Picture 33: Basic Temple Design with Two Pylons.

Picture 34: The Per-Aah (Pharaoh) Djehutimes IIII (Thothmosis) makes offerings to the Great Heru m Akhet (Sphinx)

The commemorative panel above was found between the forelegs of the Great Sphinx. It commemorates a dream experienced by Djehutimes in which Ra-Herakhti (Herukhuti, Heruakhuti) came to him and offered him kingship and sovereignty over the world if Djehutimes will repair him (the sphinx) and make devout offerings and worship. Having complied with the wishes of God, to maintain the great monument and sustained the worship of Ra-Herakhti, Djehutimes became king and Egypt prospered under his reign with the favor of God.

The Stellar Symbolism related to the Pole Star and the Opening of the mouth and Eyes Ceremony in Ancient Egypt

In his book of history, Herodotus quoted one of his guides as having told him that in Egyptian history had lasted for a period of time in which,

> "the sun had twice risen where it now set, and twice set where it now rises." This remark Schwaller de Lubicz interpreted as a description of the passage of one and a half precessional cycles. This would place the date of foundation around 36,000 BC, a date in broad agreement with the other sources."

There are three constellations that circulate around the north pole of the planet earth. These are Draco, Ursa Major and Ursa Minor. The Great Pyramid was discovered to have a shaft that point to the North Pole. Precession is the slow revolution of the Earth's axis of rotation (wobbling) about the poles of the ecliptic. A great circle inscribed on a terrestrial globe inclined at an approximate angle of 23°27' to the equator and representing the apparent motion of the sun in relation to the earth during a year. It is caused by lunar and solar perturbations acting on the Earth's equatorial bulge and causes a westward motion of the stars that takes around 25,868 years to complete. During the past 5000 years the line of direction of the North Pole has moved from the star Thuban, or Alpha (a) Draconis, in the constellation Draco, to within one degree of the bright star Polaris, also known as Alpha (a) Ursae Minoris, in the constellation Ursa Minor (Little Dipper), which is now the North Star. Polaris is a binary star of second magnitude, and is located at a distance of about 300 light-years from the earth. It is easy to locate in the sky because the two stars opposite the handle in the bowl of the dipper in the constellation Ursa Major (Big Dipper), which are called the Pointers, point to the star Polaris.

Picture 35: The Great Pyramid of Egypt with the Mystical Constellations (view from the East).

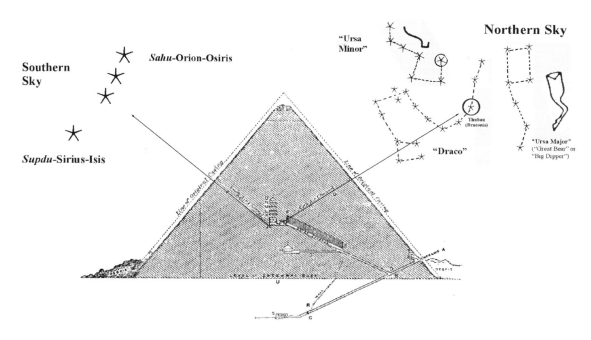

Picture 36: The Great Pyramid of Egypt with the Mystical Constellations (view from the South).

Viewed from the south the northern shaft leading from the main chamber in the great pyramid (far right) points to the point in space where there is no movement. A simulated time-lapse photo of the northern sky produces a circular motion and starlight appears as streaks across the background of the darkness of outer space. The closer one moves towards the pole the stars appear to "move" less, that is in smaller circles until at the very center there is no movement at all. This center is of course an abstract point which transcends time and space.

The changing nature of the "Pole Star" indicates that the philosophy related to the "imperishable" stars is not a physical location but rather a mystical one. The abode that is the goal of all souls is not in the stars but rather in that place where no changes or fluctuations occur, the absolute. The term used for this region in the Prt M Hru (Book of Coming into the Light) is *Yanrutf*. Yanrutf (**N-rutef** -*Nerutef*) refers to the mythological site of the grave of Asar or the innermost shrine. Yanrutf also signifies that which is in the place where nothing grows.

Opening of the Mouth with the Imperishable Stars

In the Hermetic Texts, which are the later development in Ancient Egyptian scripture, Hermes, the Greek name ascribed to the Ancient Egyptian god Djehuti, states to his pupil Asclepius (Egyptian Imhotep) that *"Did you know, O Asclepius, that Egypt is made in the image of heaven?"* The Ancient Egyptian Pyramid Texts and the Pert M Heru (Book of Enlightenment) texts contain more references to stellar mysticism. The stellar symbolism of Ancient Egypt relates to the passage of time but also to mystical awakening and spiritual realization.

> As to these all, Maat and Djehuti, they are with Isdesba Lord of Amentet. As to the divine beings behind Asar, they are again Mseti, Hapy, Duamutf, and Kebsenuf. They are behind the Chepesh in the northern heavens.
>
> From Prt M Hru Chap. 4, V. 22

The Chepesh has important mystical symbolism. Mythically it represents the foreleg of the god Set which was torn out and thrown into the heavens by the god Heru during their epic battle. A similar teaching occurs in the Babylonian epic of Gilgemesh when the "foreleg of the Bull of Heaven" is ripped out and thrown at the goddess Ishtar, who was the goddess or Queen of Heaven in Mesopotamia. It symbolizes the male generative capacity and is one of the offerings of Hetep given in Chapter 36 (usually referred to as #30B) of the Pert M Heru. Its cosmic and mystical implications provides us with insight into Kemetic philosophy as well as ancient history.

Also, in ancient times the Chepesh symbol represented the "Northern path" of spiritual evolution. Since the constellation of the Ursa Major ("Great Bear" or "Big Dipper"), known to the Ancient Egyptians as "Meskhetiu," contains **seven** stars and occupied the location referred to as the "Pole Star," it does not move, while all the other stars in the sky circle around it. This constellation, whose symbol is the foreleg, ⌐⌂, was thus referred to as "the imperishables" in the earlier Pyramid Texts: "He (the king-enlightened initiate) climbs to the sky among the imperishable stars."

𓇳𓏤𓂓𓃀𓊪𓈖✶ ✶✶Akhemu Seku - never setting stars – imperishable

𓇳𓃀𓈖𓏤𓏤𓏤𓈗𓂧𓊪𓁐✶𓏲𓏤Akhemu Urdu - never resting stars – setting

The Great Pyramid in Egypt, located in the area referred to as "The Giza Plateau" in modern times, incorporated this teaching. The main chamber in the Great Pyramid incorporates two shafts that pointed in ancient times, to the Chepesh (Ursa (Bear) Major (Great) - the foreleg) in the north sky and to Orion (Sahu or Sah), the star system of Asar (Osiris) in the southern sky. The imperishable constellation refers to that which is unchanging, absolute, transcendental and perfect.

Picture 37: The Perishable and Imperishable stars.

When the Great Pyramids are viewed over the course of one evening, from the south to north, the perishable stars (forming circles, moving below the horizon) moving around the center and the imperishable stars in the center, which do not set, that is go below the horizon, can be seen.

Time lapse photographs of this constellation show it as remaining in the center and other stars moving around it. Also, it does not sink below the horizon and become "reborn" in the eastern horizon each day as other stars. The Orion constellation refers to that which is changing, incarnating (rising in the east) and becoming. In this manner Asar is reborn through Sopdu (the star Sirius-Aset, Isis) in the form of Heru-Sopdu (Heru who is in Isis) also known as Sirius B. Therefore, mystically, the "Northern Path" is promoted as the path to immortality and enlightenment through the attainment of absolute consciousness which transcends the perishable and ever-changing nature of creation. The "Southern Path" is the process of reincarnation, renewal and repeated embodiment (*uhem ankh*), for the purpose of further spiritual evolution through self-discovery by means of human experiences. This teaching is also reflected in the zodiac inscription from the temple of Hetheru at Denderah and in the "Opening of the Mouth ceremony" where a symbol of the imperishable constellation, ⤸, is carried by the priest. The mystical intent is to open the mind, through mystical wisdom and

disciplines, so as to render it *ur-uadjit*, ⊙ , (universal and infinite, all-encompassing, unlimited) and beyond the fluctuations of egoism, i.e. mortal consciousness.

Picture 38: Below left- The Chepesh (foreleg) with constellation. Right- The Chepesh as part of the Hetep offering in the Pert M Heru Texts and temple inscriptions.

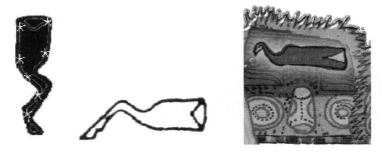

Picture 39: The Hetep Offering Slab with the foreleg symbol.

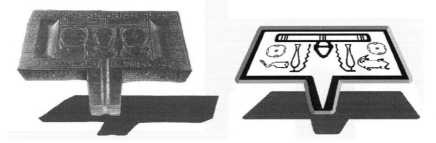

Used in the Hetep (Hotep) offering table, the leg symbolizes the male gender. The goose symbolizes the female gender. Thus, the initiate offers duality in the form of sex awareness to the divinity in exchange for the realization of nod-duality, or the transcendence of gender (dual) consciousness altogether, i.e. the "imperishable" or eternal realization of the Higher Self.

Picture 40: Vignettes from the Opening of the Mouth Ceremonies from the Ancient Egyptian texts. Left- with Chepesh (Chpsh-foreleg), Right with the Seba (Sba) ur instruments.

"O Initiate, I have come in search of you, for I am Horus; I have struck your mouth for you, for I am your beloved son; I have split open your mouth for you... I have split open your eyes for you... with the Chepch of the Eye of Heru-Chepesh (Foreleg). I have split open your mouth for you... I have split open your eyes for you... with the adze of Upuaut..... with the adze of iron . . . [PT 11-13]

The opening of the mouth and eyes is a mystical teaching relating to expansion in expression (mouth) and awareness (open eyes). These factors (mouth and eyes) are the signs of the existence of consciousness or its absence. From the passages above we learn that the priests and priestesses "open" the mouth and eyes by toughing them with the ritual instruments which symbolize the eternal, the absolute, i.e. the expansion of consciousness immortality and spiritual enlightenment. Also, we learn that the adze instrument (ursa minor) is actually also the Eye of Heru, which is the greatest offering-eucharist of the Egyptian mysteries. The Eye symbolizes divine consciousness as it is one and the same with Heru, Asar and Ra. Therefore, being touched with these instruments means attaining god-consciousness.

The Trinities of Anu

In the myth of Ra and Aset, Ra says: "I am Kheperi in the morning, and Ra at noonday, and Temu in the evening." Thus we have *Kheper-Ra-Tem,* ⊙△🝊𓏏, as the Anunian Triad and hekau. In Chapter 4 of the *Prt m Hru*, the initiate identifies {him/her}self with Tem, symbolizing that {his/her} life as a human being with human consciousness is coming to an end. Instead of an awareness of individuality and human limitation, there is now a new awareness of infinity and immortality, even though the physical body continues to exist and will die in the normal course of time. The initiate will live on as a "living" soul and join with Tem (individual consciousness joins Cosmic Consciousness):

"I am Tem in rising; I am the only One; I came into being with Nu. I am Ra who rose in the beginning."

Picture 41: The Trinity of Ta-Atum – From left to right-Khepra-Ra-Atum

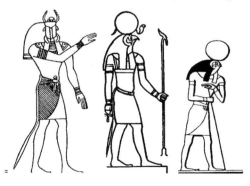

This passage is very important because it establishes the mystical transcendence of the initiate who has realized {his/her} "oneness" and union with the Divine. In other papyri, Tem is also identified with the young Harmachis (young Heru, the solar child) as the early morning sun. Thus, Kheperi-Ra-Temu are forms of the same being and are the object of every initiate's spiritual goal. Being the oldest of the three theologies, the Mysteries of Anu formed a foundation for the unfoldment of the teachings of mystical spirituality which followed in the mysteries of Hetkaptah, through Ptah, and the Mysteries of Thebes, through Amun. With each succeeding exposition, the teaching becomes more and more refined until it reaches its quintessence in the Hymns of Amun.

On the following page: Picture 42: Nefertem

Heru the Child, Nefertem, bringing forth Creation, the lotus, which springs forth from the Primeval Ocean.

In relation to the child and solar mysticism, the iconography of Nefertem is instructive. Nefertem means the beautiful or good completion, i.e., Creation has been created and brought to a conclusion through the young solar divinity. Nefertem is therefore that sun which emerges as a child emerges from the dark womb in order to create the new day. Nefertem brings creation forth by means of speech, specifically by uttering the name of all things. As modern physics informs us, all matter vibrates at a particular level. Music research also reveals that sound vibrates. The mysticism of the teachings instructs us in the wisdom that sound is controlled by mind and mind is composed of undifferentiated consciousness and consciousness is essentially the all-pervasive Spirit. Thus, in order to affect matter it is simply necessary to affect its vibrations and this can be done by uttering certain sounds with the desired intent. God intended to create Creation and thus uttered its own name and Creation came into being. Let us not forget that Creation is composed of the Nun or primeval matter which transformed itself into the Pautti. Therefore, Creation and God are one and the same.

Bronze statue of Nefertem

The Iconography of the Hawk and the Triune Form of Heru

Ancient Egyptian iconography, the pictographic elements of scripture, can independently provide deep mythological, religious and philosophical teachings by themselves. This is one of the greatest strengths of Kemetic scripture and art. This is because the reading process need not be limited to the deciphering of letters, but it can also derive meaning from pictures used in the language (pictures used as letters).

One of the most important iconographies of Kemetic religion involves the Hawk icon. The hawk is an animal which flies high above the earth and whose visual acuity allows it to survey vast regions while being able to focus on minute objects. Also, it is able to fly at high speeds. These qualities are what motivated the Ancient Egyptian Sages to use it as a symbol for the basis of the entire system of Anunian mythology which blends the concept of Tem, the singular essence which emerged out of the Primeval Void (Primeval Ocean) with the concept of Heru, the Supreme Divinity. The Hawk theme runs through the mythology of Tem as Atem-Ra or Ra-Tem, as well as that of Asar and that of Heru.

The Hawk motif unites and binds the mythology of Ra, Asar and Heru in a very strong way, and we are to understand that we are indeed looking at the same divinity who is manifesting in different aspects and operating in different realms or planes of existence. Ra represents perfection in the heavens or the transcendental, Asar Seker represents perfection in the Netherworld and Heru represents perfection in the Physical plane.

Ra, Asar and Heru

Ra represents the Divine Self, the source from which Creation arises. However, he is a High God who is the visible and dynamic expression of the formless and timeless Primeval Ocean, Nun. In any case he is still the singular essence of Creation. When he creates the other divinities it is only then that Creation comes into being.

Picture 43: The Hawk (Heru) Trinity: Ra, Asar-Sokkar and Heru

Left- Ra Herakti, Center-Asar Seker, Right- Heru, son of Asar and Aset, Lord of the Two Lands.

Ra is also related to the nameless and formless concept of the Supreme Being which transcends time and space known as **Heru**. Heru (Divinity - The Sun Divinity). Heru is the original pre-dynastic form of the Supreme Being associated with the transcendental Divinity. Heru means "The Supreme One who is above" or "That which is above." Heru (God) and Hethor (Hathor - the house of Heru) were among the first divinities to be worshipped generally throughout Ancient Egypt and as such, were the first theological expression of the duality of existence. The Supreme Being (Heru or Hor) lives within his own house (Het), the universe. Thus, God (spirit) and Goddess (creation) are in reality one and the same. In the pyramid texts, at the beginning of the Dynastic Period, the symbol of Heru, $\textinline$, is used interchangeably with ⌐, Pa Neter.

The Divine Name, Heru, is related to the word for face, Her or Hera. The relation to face implies the idea that what is above (the sky, the heavens) is the mask of the Supreme Divinity. God cannot be seen but his mask, the physical universe, can be seen.

The god Horus has several important aspects in Ancient Egyptian Mystical philosophy. In the Anunian Creation myth of the Pauti Heru is incorporated as *Heru-ur* or "Horus the aged." In the Ausarian Resurrection myth the idea of Heru (Supreme One above) was incorporated into the myth as *Heru-sa-Ast-sa Asar* (Horus, the son of Isis and Osiris). In dynastic times Heru was associated with Horus as in the Osirian Mystery where he was represented in the form of *Heru-p-khart* or "Horus the child," who later becomes Min, the *avenger of his father*.

The relationship between Ra, Asar and Heru is extremely important in the study of Anunian Mystical Philosophy and The Ausarian Resurrection Myth. It is important to not only study the scriptures relating to the mysticism but the iconography needs careful study as well since the images sometimes convey teachings not contained in the texts and also messages that cannot be conveyed in text form.

The symbol of Heru (The One Above) is the hawk or falcon bird Hieroglyphs 4. Hawks and falcons belong to the family of birds known as *Falconiformes*. Falconiformes are an order of predatory birds, comprised of vultures, kites, eagles, hawks, ospreys, falcons.[1] Falcons possess special attributes. They have keen eyesight. They can fly at fast speeds. They have streamlined bodies, hooked bills for tearing meat and strong legs with hooked claws for killing and carrying their prey. A spiritual aspirant needs to develop determination, strength, physical health, and the ability to tear asunder the vail of ignorance and the negative aspects of the mind with the claws of wisdom, righteousness and goodwill. Hieroglyphs 5, 6, 7 and 8 are some of the most ancient renditions of Heru. Hieroglyph 9 is of *Ra-Harakty* or the combination of Horus and Ra.

Hieroglyph 4:   Hieroglyph 5:

Hieroglyph 6:   Hieroglyph 7:   Hieroglyph 8:

Hieroglyph 9:

The figure below shows an Ancient Egyptian picture of Ra. His distinguishing features are the head of a Hawk bird and the body of a man. His head is surmounted by a sundisk which is encircled by a serpent (Uadjit (Udjat)-Hetheru). He holds the Uas scepter (spiritual power) and also the Ankh (life). One more important feature is the bull's tail. The tail symbolizes that Ra is the "Bull of Creation." The Bull sires the Seven Cows of Creation and the Seven Cows are the goddesses which constitutes all existence, the manifested universe. Also, Osiris is known as the Bull of Creation as well. Thus, Ra-Heru is the source and sustenance of Creation. In the center of the figure below is a picture of Asar (Osiris) in his aspect as the king of the realm of the dead. This form of Asar is known as Sokkar or Seker. His main distinguishing features are the human body with mummy wrappings and the head of the falcon with the *deshret* or white crown of Upper Egypt (heart and origin of the country). In the right of the figure below is a picture of Horus (Heru), the son of Isis and Osiris. His distinguishing features are again the head of a falcon with the body of a man. He has the *wereret* crown symbolizing the union of upper and lower Egypt (Union of the higher and the lower self), the Ankh, Uas scepter and the bull tail.

So it is clear to see by the iconography that the image of Heru is perfectly reflected in Creation through the manifestations of Ra, Asar and Heru. In this respect Ra may be seen as representing the Trinity manifestation of the spirit (Heru) in the following manner. Ra is the manifestation of the Divine in the transcendental realm (Causal Plane). Asar Seker is the manifestation of the Divine in the Netherworld (astral Plane, and Heru, the son of Asar and Aset is the manifestation of the Divine in the Earth (Physical plane. This scheme may be further defined as follows.

Heru
(That which is imperceptible, formless, timeless and absolute, transcending all planes of consciousness while at the same time permeating them as the very essence or substratum which sustains them.)

⬇

Ra
(The primordial singular essence, the soul of Creation, the first principle of manifestation by the Divine Self into the realm of time and space. In this aspect Ra symbolizes the Causal Plane of existence and consciousness.)

⬇

Asar
(As the king of the realm of the dead Asar symbolizes the Astral Plane of existence and consciousness.)

⬇

Heru-sa-Aset-sa-Asar
(The ultimate manifestation of the Divine within Creation. In this aspect Horus symbolizes the Physical Plane of existence and consciousness.)

A Hymns to Ra and Its Philosophical Principles

The following hymn is from the *Pert M Heru* or "Book of Enlightenment" from Ancient Egyptian Anunian Theology. In following its teaching it is possible to derive great wisdom and mystical insight into the nature of Ra and Anunian Theology.

Hymns to Ra

Behold Asar_____ bringing divine offerings of all the gods and goddesses. Asar _____ speaks thus:

Homage to thee, who comes in the form of Khepri, Khepri the Creator of the gods and goddesses. You rise and shine, illuminating your mother, goddess Nut, the sky, crowned as king of the gods and goddesses. Your mother Nut worships you with her two arms. The western horizon receives you in peace and Maat embraces you at the double season. Give Asar

_____ Glorious Spirit being, and spiritual strength through righteous speaking. Grant the ability to come forth as a living soul so that Asar _____ may see Heru of the two Horizons. Grant this to the Ka of Asar _____ who is Righteous of Speech in the presence of Asar, the Divine Self. Asar _____ says: Hail to all the gods and goddesses, weighers of the house of the soul, in heaven and on earth by means of the scales of Maat, who are givers of Life Force sustenance.

Tatunen, One, maker of men and women as well as the company of the gods and goddesses of the south, the north, the west and the east, i.e. all the neteru, grant praises to Ra, the lord of heaven, sovereign of life, vitality and health, maker of the gods and goddesses. Adorations to thee in your form as all goodness, as you rise in your boat. The beings up high praise thee. Beings in the lower realms praise thee. Djehuti and Maat have written for thee, who are shining forth, every day. Your enemies are put to the fire. The fiends are put down, their arms and legs being bound securely for Ra. The children of weakness disrespect and insurrection shall not continue.

The great house is in festival time. The voices of the participants are in the great temple. The gods and goddesses are rejoicing. They see Ra in his glorious rising, his beams of light piercing, inundating the lands. This exalted and venerable god journeys on and unites with the land of Manu, the western horizon, illuminating the land of his birth every day and at the same time he reaches the province where he was yesterday.

Be in peace with me! I see your beauties and I prosper upon the land; I smile and I defeat the ass fiend as well as the other fiends. Grant that I may defeat Apep in his time of strength and to see the pilot fish of the Divine Boat of Ra, which is in its blessed pool. I see Heru in the form as the guardian of the rudder. Djehuti and Maat are upon his two arms. Received am I in the prow of the Mandet Boat and in the stern of the Mesektet Boat. Ra gives divine sight, to see the Aten, to view the moon god unceasingly, every day, and the ability of souls to come forth, to walk to every place they may desire. Proclaim my name! Find him in the wood board of offerings. There have been given to me offerings in the life-giving presence, like it is given to the followers of Heru. It is done for me in the divine place in the boat on the day of the sailing, the journey of The God. I am received in the presence of Asar in the land of truth speaking of the Ka of Asar

_____.

Philosophical Principles of the Hymn to Ra

The invocatory hymn of any scripture is an important part of the overall feeling of the spiritual tradition. Ra, of course, symbolizes the Higher Self, the Supreme Being, God. Thus, the invocation to God is a form of prayer, or devotional expression towards the Divine, but at the same time it is a form of propitiation. In essence, prayer can be understood as talking to God, but the hymn goes a step further. Most times in modern culture people pray in order to ask for something. Sometimes people want God to help them with a problem in their life. Sometimes the prayer is for good luck. Sometimes the prayer is asking for the right numbers to the lottery. At other times the prayer is for deliverance from some ordeal in life. But how often do people pray for deliverance from human life? How often do people ask God to show them the way to achieve spiritual enlightenment? This is the very objective of the Hymn to Ra.

The hymn opens with salutations and descriptive appellations of Ra, as he rises in the morning. This is not some distant God, but a familiar presence. Ra is a being who can be seen daily and who can be approached easily. He illumines all the earth and causes all life to be. Ra is the source from which all of the gods and goddesses, all life, all human beings, etc., emanate. He sustains Creation by establishing Maat (order) and Djehuti (reason) as he moves through

Creation. It is especially acknowledged that Ra is not only the illuminer of the physical world, but also of the Netherworld, the Duat (kingdom of the dead). This signifies that Ra is not the sun itself. This is a very important point to understand. Ancient Egyptian mythology holds that there are three realms of existence. These are the Physical Plane (Ta), the Astral Plane (Duat) and the Heaven (Pet). Just as the universe has three realms, the human being has three bodies. These are the Physical Body, the Astral Body and the Causal Body. The physical realm is the place where human beings experience the physical body and the sense organs. The astral realm is where the mind and subtle senses operate. The Causal Body is the deep unconscious level of the mind where impressions related to one's past experiences and desires for the future are stored.

The three bodies are related to three states of consciousness within a human being or the mode in which consciousness manifests within the mind. The Physical Body relates to waking, day to day consciousness. The Astral Body relates to dream consciousness and the Causal Body relates to the unconscious level of mind. However, there is a fourth state of consciousness. This is the Transcendental Self (Neberdjer-Asar) which supports the other three (Amun-unconscious, Ra-dream and Ptah-waking). Deep within the unconscious mind lies the Self which transcends all bodies. This is the abode of Asar within every human being. If a person does not discover Asar within themselves by discovering the inner recesses of their own heart, they become caught in an endless search for fulfillment in the astral and physical realms through the astral and physical bodies. This is known as the cycle of birth and death or reincarnation. When the physical body ceases to exist, the soul of a human being goes to the astral realm in order to continue the journey of spiritual evolution.

If a person has acted with virtue and in accordance with the voice of their conscience, their soul will experience positive conditions in the astral realm. This condition is referred to as heaven. If a person acted according to their egoistic desires, selfishness and pride, they will experience pain and sorrow in the astral realm. This condition is referred to as hell. So the hymn goes on to invoke the grace of Ra. The astral realm is a subtle universe which is in a different plane than the physical. Ra passes through the astral realm just as he also passes through the physical. He passes through the physical realm in his Andetet Barque (boat), and through the astral realm in the Sekhet night barque. However, when he passes through the Duat, there are certain ropes which hang from his boat. The desire of the spiritual aspirant reading the text is that {he/she} may be able to see and grab hold of the ropes which are hanging from the boat.

The ropes symbolize divine compassion and divine love. God is extending his hand, as it were, to rescue the soul from the suffering that can occur outside of the boat. The boat itself is the innermost realm of God. It is the place of contentment and peace, being closest to the Divine. All other realms are as if a separation from that divine perfection that is in the boat. They represent a distancing from God, a separation from what is Divine.

The act of reaching out to grab the ropes is the act of spiritual aspiration and it signifies the practice of all of the spiritual disciplines (of Yoga) which enable a person to move towards their Higher Self as opposed to getting more deeply involved in the relative realms which are again, a separation from the Divine.

This is a beautiful hymn dedicated to the Divine, the Supreme Being, in the form of Ra. It contains much of the same feeling and dedications as in Plate 1 of the papyrus of Ani. However, it also has several important additional teachings which are important to the study of Pert Em Heru.

The idea of Ra emerging and "inundating the lands" with his life giving essence has special mystical significance. This teaching refers to the original creation when the entire universe and the forms of Creation were not yet in existence. The time prior to the dawn symbolizes the undifferentiated state of the universe as well as the human mind. In the beginning the universe was like a calm ocean and there was no differentiation in it. Everything looked the same. However, when Ra emerged from the ocean he caused waves, and these waves took on many different forms. These forms are what we refer to as elements or matter. Think of the time when you fall asleep. You lose consciousness of your waking personality and you are submerged in an ocean without forms. This is like the primeval ocean of creation. From it arises your dream world in which you are a character among other characters of your own creation. Thus, you are the Creator of your dream world and God is the creator of the dream of the universe.

God created the universe by causing vibrations in that primordial ocean of his own consciousness by uttering sound. Sound is the medium by which God ordains what happens in Creation from its inception to its end. The word manifests through the power and faculty of speech. Therefore, speech is related to Cosmic Consciousness and the ability to create in the world of time and space as well as in the astral realm. In the same manner, a human being can create his or her world according to the desire of the heart.

Thus, just as a human being must breathe air in order to sustain life, this entire universe must receive the breath of life from the Divine in order to be sustained. However, ordinary human beings (ignorant masses) only know of the physical air that sustains the physical body. A spiritual aspirant seeks to breath the air which sustains the elevated states of consciousness which are above the waking state of consciousness.

The hymn goes on to show that Ani praises the Divine at dawn and at eventide. This teaching relates to the necessity for devotional exercise such as prayers, chanting and recitation of the hekau or words of power which propitiate divine grace and promote spiritual knowledge and the kindling of spiritual feeling deep within the heart leading to purity and enlightenment. A person engages constantly in the world with its illusions. Thus, spiritual practice should be daily, encompassing every aspect of life, in order to overwhelm the worldly impressions produced by distraction, ignorance and the lower desires. The process of spiritual worship leads a human being to draw divine grace to {him/her} self. This is what is referred to as being one of the "favored ones" of God. This favored status is attained by becoming "one of those who worshipped thee upon earth" meaning while they were alive and in human form.

Many people mistakenly believe that the Pert Em Heru is a book of rituals only for people who have passed on to the next life, but in reality it is a discipline for those who are alive. The physical body is the best place to carry out a spiritual program, the practice of Yoga and Mystical Religion. This is because it is the place where the soul can experience an extended period of waking consciousness in which to consciously work on purifying the heart. The dream and dreamless sleep states or subconscious and unconscious levels of the mind are inconstant and minimal spiritual progress can be accomplished in these states.

Ra and Aton and the Philosophy of Akhenaton

Many writers have striven to show Atenism, the philosophy of Akhenaton, as a new innovation, as separate and deviant from the rest of Ancient Egyptian mythology and philosophy. However, upon closer examination, the philosophy of Atonism is quite closely related to Anunian Theology. This is because they had the same common origins and any differences are of degrees of expressing a particular aspect of theology over others at a given time. There are no fundamental differences between Atonism and other religious traditions of Ancient Egypt. The teachings presented in the Hymn to Ra will be noticeably similar to those in the Hymns to Aton (Above). Further, their similarity with the Vedic and Hindu solar conceptions will become evident.

The Hymns to Aton and Their Philosophical Principles

When the hymns to Aton and Ra are compared closely it is discovered that they are both referring to the same divinity. A better way of understanding this is that the worship of Aton was actually the worship of Ra in a more ancient form, highlighting certain features or attributes of Ra in the form of Herakhti. This understanding of course helps us to realize that what on the surface appears to be a disparity or deviation in the practice of Ancient Egyptian religion is actually quite in keeping with the tradition, as the worship of the divine in its various forms was part of the tradition since the earliest times.

Hymns to Aton by Akhenaton

A- The fish in the river swim towards thy face, thy beams are in the depths of the Great Green (i.e., the Mediterranean and Red Seas). The earth becometh light, thou shootest up in the horizon, shining in the Aten in the day, thou scatterest the darkness.

Explanation: Philosophical Principle

A-From time immemorial God was worshipped as the Sun in Ancient Egypt. This has prompted many scholars in ancient and modern times, ignorant of the metaphorical symbolism, to refer to their worship as idolatry. This verse shows that God is seen as the principle operating through the sun and not the sun itself.

———————————

B- Thou makest offspring to take form in women, creating seed in men. Thou makest the son to live in the womb of his mother, making him to be quiet that he crieth not, thou art a nurse in the womb, giving breath to vivify that which he hath made.

Explanation: Philosophical Principle

B- God is not only the Creator of human life but also the very Life Force that sustains it. Worldly people would see the mother as sustaining the baby in the womb. Akhenaton affirms the higher source of sustenance i.e. God. The exact word used is "vivify." God is therefore not remote but intimately involved with Creation.

———————————

C- *[When] he droppeth from the womb on the day of his birth [he] openeth his mouth in the [ordinary] manner, thou providest his sustenance…The young bird in the egg speaketh in the shell, thou givest breath to him inside it to make him to live. Thou makest for him his mature form so that he can crack the shell [being] inside the egg. He cometh forth from the egg, he chirpeth with all his might, when he hath come forth from it (the egg), he walketh on his two feet.*

Explanation: Philosophical Principle

C- The philosophy of "breath" or breath of life has a very important teaching behind it. Breath relates to the Life Force energy, which vivifies everything. The force is subtle and thus interpenetrates all creation, thereby enlivening and sustaining it from within, much like the later Holy Spirit of the Bible. There is a recognition here that it is this same force, which causes vegetation and human life to grow and thrive.

D- *One God, like whom there is no other. Thou didst create the earth by thy heart (or will), thou alone existing, men and women, cattle, beasts of every kind that are upon the earth, and that move upon feet (or legs), all the creatures that are in the sky and that fly with their wings, [and] the deserts of Syria and Kush (Nubia), and the Land of Egypt.*

Explanation: Philosophical Principle

D- This important verse brings forth the understanding that there is a Supreme Being above the gods and goddesses. God caused all to come into being by his will and is not just the Creator of what exists (nature, living beings etc.) but that God and Creation are indeed one and the same, "alone existing" in the form of or manifesting as animals, people of all lands, etc.

E- *Thou settest every person in his place. Thou providest their daily food, every man having the portion allotted to him; [thou] dost compute the duration of his life. Their tongues are different in speech, their characteristics (or forms), and likewise their skins (in color), giving distinguishing marks to the dwellers in foreign lands… Thou makest the life of all remote lands.*

Explanation: Philosophical Principle

E- God has Created all peoples, all nations and countries and has appointed each person's country of residence, language and even their ethnicity and physical appearance or features. So all people, including those of foreign lands, have the same Creator and owe their continued existence to the same Divine Being.

F- *Oh thou Lord of every land, thou shinest upon them…*

Explanation: Philosophical Principle

F- In no uncertain terms, there is one God (Lord) who is the Supreme Being of all countries.

G- Thou hast made millions of creations from thy One self (viz.) towns and cities, villages, fields, roads and river. Every eye (i.e., all men) beholdeth thee confronting it. Thou art the Aton of the day at its zenith.

G- God manifests as and in countless forms, indeed, everything that exists, including life forms but also inanimate objects as well. Thus, when a person uses their senses and perceives objects, they are in reality perceiving God who is manifesting as Creation. This realization indicates the attainment of the highest goals of spiritual realization. This attainment is also known as non-dual vision, seeing God everywhere without separation between Creation and Divinity or the soul from God. This is of course the same teaching given by Jesus in the Gnostic Gospel of Thomas from Egypt where he asserts that "The Kingdom is spread upon the earth but people do not see it!"

The Nondualist Philosophy of Akhenaton

On the surface, a preliminary examination of Akhenaton's teaching would seem to indicate that the system of worship which he instituted was a "new religion" or a "departure" from established traditions. Actually, In instituting the worship of Aton, Akhenaton was actually reviving the form of ancient worship that had been related to Ra in the form of Herakhti. This perspective is evident in the title that he chose for himself as well as the hymns to Aton which make reference to the Divine as

"the high priest of Herakhti who is in the horizon in his name of Shu who is in the Aton."

Thus, we find that Atonism is closely related to Herakhti and thus with the most ancient forms of the solar divinity. Further, Atonism regards the Aton or sundisk, as the body (*who is in the Aton*) but not the essence of the Divine Self. Therefore, Atonism is an attempt to express the ancient understanding of the divine as a spirit who manifests in physical form and sustains all existence. The arms and hands of the Aton thus symbolize the all-pervading nature of the solar rays which touch all and sustain all. However, the spirit who resides or works through the sundisk is the higher object of worship.

Atonism

Akhenaton was at the same time, a king and mystical philosopher. He introduced not a new religion, but a form of worship, which was highly philosophical and abstract, and thus less suited for the masses and more appropriate for the monastic order. The tenets of his hymns can be found in hymns to other Ancient Egyptian gods such as Amun (Amen), Asar (Asar), and Ra, which preceded those to Aton. However, the form of their exposition brings forth a new dimension of Ancient Egyptian philosophy, which is unsurpassed in some ways, even by the Hymns of Amun. However, he was not able to reconcile the worship of Aton with the pre-existing forms of worship in Ancient Egypt. Also, he was not able to balance the duties of kingship with those of his position as High Priest. While he was not able reconcile these issues, he did bring forth the most advanced exposition of Ancient Egyptian philosophy. Scholars of religious studies have classified him as the first monotheist, before Moses, but his contributions to religion go much deeper than the simple monotheistic concept put forth by Moses.

Upon closer study, the philosophy, which Akhenaton espoused, is comparable to the most advanced spiritual philosophies developed in India, known as Vedanta philosophy. In Vedanta, two important forms of spiritual philosophy developed. They are expressions of non-dualist philosophy known as Absolute Monism. The Hymns to Aton, which also espouse Absolute Monism, were recorded at least 579 years before its exposition in India through the Hindu Upanishads which are considered to be the highest expression of Hindu mystical philosophy. Akhenaton's teachings were given less than 200 years before the supposed date for the existence of Moses. However, Moses' teaching was not understood as Absolute Monism, but rather as monotheism. Therefore, whether the Jewish Pentateuch was written by a person named Moses or by Jewish scribes much later, as most modern biblical scholars now agree, the influence of Akhenaton's teachings would have been foremost in the instruction of Moses. Remember that the Bible says Moses learned the wisdom of the Egyptians (Acts 7:22). While all of the attributes of Yahweh, the Hebrew God, are contained in the teachings related to Aton, the Hymns to Aton go farther in espousing the nature of God and God's relationship to Creation and humanity. They are based on Monism. Absolute Monism means that there is a recognition that there is only one reality that exists: God. All else is imagination. This means that everything that is perceived with the senses, thoughts, etc., is a manifestation of God. Modified Monism views God as the soul of nature, just as the human body also has a soul, which sustains it.

The next form of philosophy present in Akhenaton's hymns is Pantheism. There are two forms of Pantheism, Absolute and Modified. Absolute Pantheism views God as being everything there is. In other words, God and Creation are one. Modified Pantheism is the view that God is the reality or principle behind nature. Panentheism is the doctrine that God is immanent in all things but also transcendent, so that every part of the universe has its existence in God, but God is more than the sum total of the parts. God transcends physical existence. Aten or Aton was represented not as a human being, but as the sun, from which extended rays that terminated with hands which bestowed Ankhs (Life Force), to all Creation. This image was used exclusively and constituted a non-personalized form of Divine iconography pointing towards the abstract and transcendental nature of the Divine as a principle, as opposed to a personality. This was not a departure from Ancient Egyptian philosophy, but an attempt to reinforce elements, which were already present in the very early forms of worship, related to the formless, nameless *God of Light* teaching. The following exerted verses from the Hymns to Aten approved by Pharaoh Akhenaton exhibit the most direct exposition of the philosophies mentioned above.

Picture 44: Akhenaton with his family, receiving Life Force from Aten through the sun's rays.

One God, like whom there is no other. Thou didst create the earth by thy heart (or will), thou alone existing, men and women, cattle, beasts of every kind that are upon the earth, and that move upon feet (or legs), all the creatures that are in the sky and that fly with their wings, [and] the deserts of Syria and Kush (Nubia), and the Land of Egypt.

Thou settest every person in his place. Thou providest their daily food, every man having the portion allotted to him; [thou] dost compute the duration of his life. Their tongues are different in speech, their characteristics (or forms), and likewise their skins (in color), giving distinguishing marks to the dwellers in foreign lands... Thou makest the life of all remote lands.

Oh thou Lord of every land, thou shinest upon them...

Thou hast made millions of creations from thy One self (viz.) towns and cities, villages, fields, roads and river. Every eye (i.e., all men) beholdeth thee confronting it (the objects of the world).

These statements by Akhenaton in his Hymns to Aton follow the transcendental and tantric philosophy that originated in the *Pyramid* and *Coffin Texts,* and much later, in the Gnostic Gospels which was espoused by Jesus. Nature itself and all objects including people are a manifestations of the Divine.

> *"The Kingdom is spread upon the earth but people do not see it!"*
> –Jesus in the Gnostic Gospel of Thomas from Egypt

In the New Testament *Gospel of Luke* 17:21 we find the following statement:

> *"The Kingdom of God is in the midst of you (within thee)."*
> –Jesus in the Christian Bible

Anunian Theology and its relation to other Ancient Egyptian Theologies

The Mysteries of Anu are considered to be the oldest exposition of the teachings of Creation and they formed a foundation for the unfoldment of the teachings of mystical spirituality which followed in the mysteries of the city of *Hetkaptah* through the Divinity in the name Ptah, and the Mysteries of *Newt (Waset or Thebes)*, through the Divinity in the name Amun. With each succeeding exposition, the teaching becomes more and more refined until it reaches its quintessence in the *Hymns of Amun.* Thus, while each of the divinities in the Ancient Egyptian Trinity (Amun-Ra-Ptah) are related, in their own tutelary way they assume the form of the *High Divinity* or *Supreme Being* with name and form. However, as we have seen, they are only representations or symbols (representation with name and form) of the transcendental androgynous Divinity which is without name or form who is referred to as Neberdjer. This understanding holds vast implications for the comprehension of Ancient Egyptian Religion and its message in reference to the human soul because the human soul is related to Neberdjer just as the Trinity is related to Neberdjer. How is this possible? This is the teaching of the Hymns of Amun.

The concept behind the teaching of Amun is the central theme of not only Ancient Egyptian Religion and mystical philosophy, but also of every world religion and of modern physics as well. The idea of Amun has been mythologized by Sages in such a fashion that the continuous study of the teachings and myths reveal increasingly more profound layers of the mystery of life. The outer layers are shed through understanding of the philosophical ideas and teachings. When understanding reaches an intuitive level through the study and practice of the teachings, the core wherein lies the discovery of the true essence of mystical religious philosophies is revealed.

The name *Amun* appears in the remotest times of Egyptian history and came to prominence in the ancient city of Waset (Thebes), Egypt. The mysteries of Amun represent a quintessence of Egyptian philosophy concerning the nature of the un-manifest aspect of all existence and the understanding of human consciousness. This teaching speaks of God as an un-manifest, nameless, formless *Being of Light* which is the source of all that is manifest. The formless *Being of Light* also became known as the *Nu, the Watery Abyss* and as Amun, the Witnessing Self. In the Ancient Egyptian Shabaka Inscription, this teaching was espoused with *Ptah* assuming the role of the manifestation of the un-manifest Self.

In Egypt, the concept of God, the ultimate and absolute reality-**Un maat** behind all physical manifestations, was called *Amn* or *Amun* or *Neberdjer* or *Pa Neter*. In Hindu mythology, it is *Brahman*, to the Taoists, it is *The Tao,* in Judaism it is referred to as *Yahweh*, in Islam it is *Allah*, in Christianity it is *God the Father* and *The Kingdom of Heaven,* and to modern physics it is *Energy*. In Indian mystical philosophy the inner Self is referred to as *Antar Amin*. The similarity in the terms used to denote *The Self* in Ancient Egypt and India is evident.

Since the most ancient times of Egyptian civilization, a nameless, formless, gender-less "Supreme God," was also referred to as *"Neter Neteru" (God of gods),* and as *"The Hidden One,"* until later times when myths were constructed for the understanding of the common people which made use of symbols or forms. Thus, representations of God began to appear, first in zoomorphic forms (using animals to convey a symbolic image), and then in anthropomorphic (human) forms. *"Pa Neter"* or "The God" was thought of as a Father-Mother Creator God and must not be confused with the *"neteru"* or "gods and goddesses," which represented the cosmic forces of the Universe which emanate from Pa Neter.

Prior to creating, the Creator is viewed as both female and male until creation is created, at which time creation becomes the female principle (Creation) and the mover-vivifier (God), becomes the male principle (Spirit) . This is the beginning of duality coming out of non-duality. From an advanced point of view however, God is neither male nor female, but God is the source from which the Gods and Goddesses (neteru), men and women and all creation comes. Therefore, the concept of *"Pa Neter"* encompasses a concept that goes beyond ordinary human - mental understanding of God. For the "common folk," *"Pa Neter"* was referred to as Amon - Ra - Ptah, the Holy Trinity, or as Asar, Aset, Horus, Hathor, etc., and was represented by various symbols such as the Sundisk or a single flag, as well as other symbols. These symbols contain deep mystical significance and hold formulas which convey mystical teachings about ourselves and the nature of existence.

Each divine aspect and symbol for the Divine carries with it certain specific pieces of information which, when put together through intuitive understanding, reveal the wholeness of creation and of human consciousness. Thus, through each major High God and his Consort, different levels of mystical wisdom are revealed. In three of the major cosmological systems of Ancient Egypt, mystical wisdom is revealed through the symbolic representation of the deities and through their relationships. The relationships of the deities constitute the different

"Companies" (*Paut Neteru*) of gods who are in the following of the High (Supreme) God (*Neter Neteru*). Further, the Companies reveal that the Supreme Being exists in the un-manifest form and manifests as a Trinity (*Amun-Ra-Ptah*), and also as the different principles which are represented by the various Gods and Goddesses (*Neteru*). In this manner, the ancient texts themselves proclaim that *Amun* is One and Alone, *Ptah* is One and Alone, and *Ra* is One and Alone. All deities are *One* because they represent the One Supreme Being, so there is no conflict because there are no differences between them; they are only symbols of certain characteristic principles of the same Divine Self, so their differences are of appearance only. Thus, the concept of the High God must be interpreted in a much broader sense than in the stricter dogmatic religious philosophies. The High God is androgynous, therefore, male or female deities may serve the role of High God as is needed for the particular doctrine and wisdom teaching. Thus, Amun, Ra, Ptah, Asar, Horus, Khepera, Aset, Hathor, Mut, Nut, etc., are all representatives or representations of the Supreme Deity which is beyond name and form, though manifesting with name and form.

By looking at the various deities with an insight into the principles they represent and their relationships to the absolute Supreme Being (*Pa Neter*), the correct understanding emerges with respect to the androgynous nature and origin of the soul. In ancient texts, Aset informs Horus that *sex is a thing of bodies and not of souls* and elsewhere, we are instructed that *the body belongs to the earth and the soul to heaven.* Therefore, you are to understand that the task of the mysteries of Yoga involve a shifting of your conscious identification from the body to the soul essence. With this understanding, the concept of *Pa Neter* includes the female element. So when Aset says she is *All that is and All that shall ever be* and Hathor is described as *One and Alone,* you can understand these statements as all being true.

Furthermore, all deities of other religions (Jesus, Krishna, Buddha, etc.) are *One* as well, in that they are symbols and representations of the One ultimate reality behind all names and forms. So whatever deity is chosen for worship, there is no conflict because the true object of worship is the transcendental reality behind the form of the deity. In this manner, religion progresses from the ritualistic level where the external form of the Divine is worshipped to the mythical level, wherein the particular deity is worshipped as a representation of the Divine. Finally, religious movement progresses to the metaphysical or mystical level where the deities are intentionally understood to be representations of the divine essence underlying all things, which is the innermost reality of yourself. With this understanding, the essence of God within the innermost recesses of your heart is revealed.

So any deity may be chosen according to the level of understanding and *meskhenet* (karmic) inclination of the individual. There are varied forms of religions and yoga disciplines in existence because there are varied human personalities. Further, since all things in creation are in reality manifestations of God, everything in creation is divine and is therefore worthy of deification and reverence. The goal of each and every discipline of yoga is the attainment of the beatific state of Enlightenment wherein all Creation is understood as being Divine.

The Path of the Goddess

The Goddess Aspect of Creation

The female principle is prominent in Ancient Egyptian mythology and religious iconography because there was a recognition that Creation is composed of complementary opposites. This means that Creation is a mixture of both male and female elements which cannot exist without each other. The Ancient Egyptian Sages discovered that when there is an imbalance between these principles, there is strife and unrest in human life. When there is balance and harmony, there is peace and prosperity. Therefore, the God must have his female counterpart, the Goddess, and vice versa. This teaching brings up many principles of tantric philosophy. Many of these will be discussed throughout this volume. For more information on this topic see the book *Egyptian Tantra Yoga* from the Egyptian Yoga Book Series by Dr. Muata Ashby.

An Ancient Egyptian Creation myth holds that all came into existence out of a primeval ocean of unformed matter, the Duat (Duat). The teaching of the fullness of the primeval ocean is to be found in the *Book of Coming Forth By Day* (xvii. 76,79; lxxi. 13; cxxiv. 17). The hekau-utterance in Chapter xvii gives an exact description of the concept of "fullness" and of the female nature of the primeval ocean. The initiate says:

> *"Behold Ra who was born yesterday from the buttocks of the Goddess Mehurt."*
> *In the answer to the question: "What then is this?," it is explained: "It is the watery abyss of heaven, or as others say, It is the image of the Eye of Ra in the morning at His daily birth. Mehurt is the Eye (Utchat) of Ra."*

Mehurt was originally the female embodiment of the watery matter, the primeval ocean from which the substance of the world was formed and from which Ra emerged. In other versions of the Creation story, the primeval ocean is referred to as Nu, a male form. Thus, the primeval ocean is seen as an *androgynous* essence from which all arose in the form of opposites. Mehurt, ⸺⸺⸺, means **"mighty fullness."** She symbolizes the infinite source of matter which is impregnated by the male spirit. This is one of the reasons why one of the symbols of Amun (Ancient Egyptian name for God-Supreme Being) is a pregnant woman ⸻ . Of course, the female primeval matter and the male spirit are both aspects of the same energy. This is expressed in the last line of the utterance where it is explained that Mehurt herself is the "image" of the "Eye of Ra." The Eye of Ra is Ra's own daughter, Hethor. She is his dynamic expression in the world of time and space which he projects from his abode which is outside of time and space.

Mehurt is depicted as a cow Goddess brimming with life giving essence. The symbol of the cow is also common to Hethor, Nut and Aset. The Goddess in the form of a cow is often referred to as a "seven fold deity" known as the "seven Hethors" who preside over the life of each individual and the course of Creation. This title refers to the further differentiation of the three primordial principles of the Trinity (Asar-Aset-Heru) which is expressed as the phenomenal universe through a series of sevens. This number, *seven*, is expressed in all levels of Creation. It is expressed in the seven levels of the human subtle anatomy with the seven spiritual centers,[8] and also as the seven primary colors of the rainbow. This principle of sevens translated into the Gnostic idea of the "seven planetary spirits," and the Christian Archangels, known as the *Heads of the Celestial Host,* were titled the "Seven Archangels of the Presence." Seven is also a special number to the Ancient Egyptian goddess Sesheta.

---

[8] see *Egyptian Yoga: The Philosophy of Enlightenment* and *The Serpent Power*

Aset-Hethor in Ancient Egypt symbolized the source of Creation. Her udder produced the Milky Way. She was "the Great Cow which gave birth to Ra, the Great Goddess, the mother of all the gods and goddesses...the lady who existed when nothing else had being, and who created that which came into being." The cow is therefore a prominent representation of Aset and Hethor. In her form as seven cows, Hetheru, an aspect of Aset, symbolizes the seven energies which course through the universe and which are engendered by the *Bull* (Osiris-male aspect of the Supreme Being). The *Bull* is a metaphor for the spirit. Just as the bull on a farm sires many cows, so to the "Bull" (Supreme Spirit) engenders all life in Creation.

In Indian Mythology, the cow holds a similar symbolism as that of Ancient Egypt. The cow is known as the "fountain of milk and curds." In a mystical sense, the world is a curd of the milk which emanated from the Celestial Cow (Goddess).

The Eye of Ra (𓂀) is Ra's creative principle in the female aspect. Thus, creation itself is an image of God. The primordial essence from which creation arises and that which arises as creation are images of God in much the same way as your thoughts and dreams are images of your consciousness.

Through the interplay of the male and female principles, an infinite variety of forms can arise. This is the cause of the multiplicity that is seen in creation. The multiplicity of chemical elements and the infinite varieties, shapes and forms which are possible through their combinations are in reality expressions of the two principles, the opposites, duality, which are an expressions of the one, singular and non-dual essence. All of the multiplicity is in reality an expression of the two principles (duality) which, when examined closely with keen philosophical reason and an intuitive mind, are found to be in reality a singular or non-dual principle. This is the deeper meaning of the Ancient Egyptian teaching: *I became from God one, gods three,* which was presented earlier, where God tells us he was one essence and then transformed himself into three. These three constitute the basis of the multiplicity of creation; the duality, along with the interaction between the two, make three principles. However, the substratum of all creation (the trinity and duality) is oneness and this oneness has been translated into religion as the concept of monotheism and the Trinity. However, monotheism as it is understood in Western religions such as Orthodox Christianity, Orthodox Islam, Orthodox Judaism and others, is not the same monotheism implied in the teachings of Yoga and mystical religions such as the Egyptian Mysteries, Vedanta, Sufism, Buddhism, the Tao, etc.

In Western religion, monotheism implies that there is one God who exists in fact and is watching over his creation. God is conceptualized as a male figure who is separate from creation and manages it from afar. In the mystical sciences, monotheism implies that God is the only being that truly exists and therefore all that exists is an expression of the Divine. God expresses as nature, the stars, your body, your thoughts, your senses, all physical objects, all good and evil people, etc. God is everything, just as everything in your dreams is in reality an expression of your own consciousness. God is not separate from creation, but is immanent in creation. God is never far from you, but is as close as your every thought, every breath, every sensation, every feeling. Thus, that which transcends the phenomenal world of time and space is "full" and the phenomenal world which is an expression of the eternal is also "full." At every moment you are embracing the glory of God. At every moment , regardless of your life's circumstances, you are full. Even if you were to become blind or to lose an arm or leg, you would remain full. Just as the injuries of your dream personalities do not affect you as you lay on your bed, so too your transcendental Self is unaffected by any condition that is experienced by your body or mind (ego-personality).

This exact teaching of the "fullness" of God and the "fullness" of creation may be found in the Indian Upanishads in the following prayer:

Purnamadah Purnamidam Purnat
Purnamudachyate Purnasya
Purnamadaya Purnamevavahisyate.
Om Shantih, Shantih, Shantih.*

That (Absolute) is full, this (world, being a manifestation of the Absolute) is full. When this (world-process) is taken away (by transcending it through Self-realization), what remains is full (the Absolute). May there be Peace, Peace, Peace.

On the following page: From the Step Pyramid- Ra revives the body through the Serpent Power

The Illusoriness of Creation

According to Memphite Theology and to this Hymn of Amun which constitutes Theban Theology, what is considered as solid matter is in reality nothing more than the same form of matter which is experienced in the dream state of consciousness. Thus, the "physical" world is composed of the same material as the dream world and is therefore subject to vanish as surely as a dream. However, the phenomenal world, being part of God's dream, or projection, as opposed to that of a human being, is longer lived. It may last billions of years from the standpoint of a human lifetime, however, it is only a flash in the realm of eternity. Thus, the human concept of "time" is only a minute segment within the stream of eternity. The concept of relativity of time is expressed in a hieroglyphic text entitled: *The Songs of The Harper*. In one verse, the relativity of the passage of time is explained as follows:

"The whole period of things done on the earth is but a period of a dream."

Consider your dreams. They may seem to occur over a period of hours, days, months or years. Yet upon waking up, you realize that the entire time you were in bed asleep for a short time. In the same way, the entire period of the existence of the universe is nothing but the span of a short dream in the mind of God.

From an advanced perspective, neither time nor space can be said to exist as something which is real, just as time, matter, and physical objects within a dream cannot be called "real." The entire dream world exists in the mind and does not require real time or space. The phenomenal world which is experienced in the waking state of consciousness is also not real and does not exist except in the mind of God. This teaching is not only confirmed by the Hymns of Amun, but it is also a primary teaching of Memphite Theology presented in the *Shabaka Inscription*. In reality, only eternity is real, and God is eternity. Since all matter is in reality constituted of the thought energy of God, and changes in the matter are called time, it must be clearly understood that God is the only reality which exists.

God is eternity, and the limited perceptions of the mind and senses are what human beings refer to as "time" and "space" awareness. However, the perception of time and space is due to the limitations and conditioning of the human mind and body. If you had the ability to perceive the entire universe at once, an eternal view which is not restricted to time and space, then you would discover that there is only oneness. This is the view that the cosmic mind (God) has towards creation. Recall the teachings of Memphite Theology on the creation of the universe by Ptah through thought alone. Thus, the task of the spiritual aspirant is to grow out of the limitations of the mind and body and discover the cosmic vision which lies within. When this is accomplished, there is a new perception of the universe. This represents the death of the ego in a human being and the birth of the spiritual life in the human being.

God has assumed the form of the neters or Pauti (Company of gods and goddesses). These "neters" are cosmic forces and energies that sustain the universe and which constitute "physical matter." Therefore, this "physical" universe is in reality the body of God and everything in it is Divine, from the smallest atom to the largest celestial bodies in the heavens.

Picture 45: The Goddess Net

Goddess Net

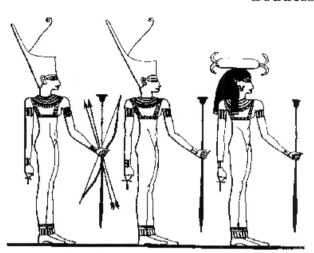

Anunian theology is intimately related to Saisian mysticism, as the goddess Net is actually the female equivalent as the divinity Ra. She is the light of all lights and the essence which gave birth to the sun (Ra). Net is also the goddess of creation and war, as well as honor and decisive action. Her attributes are the bow, shield and arrows. She is androgynous (neither male nor female), and was known to watch over Asar's ceremonial bed when he lay dead, along with Aset and Nebthet. She assisted Djehuti in bringing justice for Heru in the Asarian myth. The goddess Net is the primordial Supreme Divinity with female aspect. She is the ancient form of the goddesses Aset and Hetheru, and her worship extended to the far reaches of antiquity, into the Pre-Dynastic period of Ancient Egyptian history. There are records from both priests and priestesses who served the temples of goddess Net. These show that worship of her was most popular, and expressed generally throughout the land of Egypt in ancient times. As we will see, the teachings related to goddess Net are profound and in every way as elevated as those of the Supreme Divinities of Ancient Egypt which portray the male aspect.

In *Pyramid Text* line 606, Net, together with Aset, Nebethet and Serqet, watched over the funerary bed of Asar. The bandages and shrouds used for the mummy of the deceased was given by goddess Net and through these she imparts her protection as well as her blessings in the form of spiritual power.

In *Pyramid Text* line 620-627, it is explained that the initiate is Sebek, the god who is the son of Net, and that the initiate rises like the son of Net. In the city of Net, Sebek is recognized as a form of Heru. Therefore, there is no conflict in finding that the goddess Aset was ascribed her attributes in the later dynastic period. The following speech of the goddess is also used by goddess Aset.

> **"I am everything which has been, and which is, and which shall be and there has never been anyone who has uncovered my veil."**

Of the goddess it is said that she:

> **"Created the seed of the gods and goddesses and men and women."**

Net is the Goddess of Light, and thus her festival is characterized by the practice of lighting candles, torches and lamps. As light she gave birth to Ra, the sun divinity, who lights up the world.

Net is the:

"Divine Cow who gave birth to Ra."

Thus, Net is *Mehurt*, the primeval waters from which creation arose.

Her androgynous nature is related in the following epithet:

"Father of all fathers and mother of all mothers."

"Net-Menhit, the Great Lady, Lady of the south, the great cow who gave birth to the sun, who made the seed of the gods and goddesses and men and women, the mother of Ra, the one who raised up Tem in the primeval time, who existed when nothing else had existence and who created that which exists after she came into existence."

The goddess gave birth to the gods and goddesses and to human beings, but she herself was not given birth. She brought herself into existence and gave birth without being impregnated. She was the primeval ocean and she emerged as herself out of herself and all has come forth through and from her. She is self-existent, and her nature is secret, a mystery to all.

shetat - deep mysterious nature of the goddess Net

Net is also referred to as:

"Ua-netert"
"Divinity One"

Thus, Net encompasses the non-dual, absolute, all-encompassing divinity, i.e., she is Neberdjer. This teaching is further illustrated through the hieroglyphic symbols of her name.

Her symbols are the bow, ⌒, two arrows, ⟵, the shield, ⬚, and the knitting spool, ⋈ .

The name *Net*, ⌒, is a play on the word *nt*, ⌒ ,or *ntet*, ⌒ ⌒, meaning that which is, that which exists, i.e. that which is real, true, and abiding. The goddess provides *saa*, ⧋, or protection for the spiritual aspirant. She uses a bow and arrow to shoot down the enemies of the righteous (anger, hatred, greed, jealousy, envy, lust, etc.).

In her name of *Net hetep*, ✕⌒, the goddess is the abiding supreme peace.

Net is also known as Amentet, the hidden goddess and consort of the god Amen as well as Rat, the consort of the god Ra. Thus we are to understand that all the goddess forms are in reality aspects of Net.

Net is also known as *Mehenit*, ∼∼∼ 𓏤𓏤 ∘ 𓃀, the weaving goddess. The material woven by the goddess is used for wrapping the mummy, but she also weaves her own clothing. This clothing is the outer appearance of the physical universe. The objective of spiritual movement within the *het Net*, 𓉠 ∘ 𓉠 ⊗, the house of Net (Creation), is to propitiate the goddess to remove her clothing, to unveil herself, so that the initiate may see her true form...absolute existence.

Being the Goddess of Light and having the power to weave the intricate web of Creation wherein all is connected, the goddess allows herself to be disrobed by those who follow the path to her discovery. This path was given in the Temple of Aset, who is a later form of goddess Net. In the temple of Aset the path of spirituality (Shetaut Aset), known today as the Yoga of Wisdom, was taught. It is a spiritual discipline involving the following areas. The aspirant is to purify of the body through a vegetarian diet, control of the sex urge, engage in devotional practices and study of the wisdom teachings. **Stage 1: Listening** to the teachings of the myth of the goddess and receiving mystical insights into these. **Stage 2: Reflecting** on those teachings, and living life in accordance with virtue and truth (i.e. practice of the teachings in daily life). **Stage 3: Through Subtle One-pointed Mentation,** leading oneself to a meditative union with the Goddess who is the essence of light, which transcends mind, body, time and space.

Picture 46: Mehurt - Hetheru

The Goddess of Creation

Related to the goddess Hetheru, Mehurt was originally the female embodiment of the watery matter, the Primeval Ocean from which the substance of the world was formed and from which Ra emerged. In other versions of the Creation story, the Primeval Ocean is referred to as Nu, a male form. Thus, the Primeval Ocean is seen as an *androgynous* essence from which all arose in the form of opposites. Mehurt, ⟍𓏏𓏏𓄿 ⟍ ∘ 𓆑𓃀, means "mighty fullness." She was the infinite source of matter which was impregnated by the male spirit. This is one of the reasons why one of the symbols of Amun is a pregnant woman 𓁐 . Of course, the female primeval matter and the male spirit are both aspects of the same energy. This is expressed in the last line of the utterance where it is explained that Mehurt herself is the "image" of the "Eye of Ra." The Eye of Ra is His own daughter, Hetheru. Mehurt is depicted as a cow goddess brimming with life giving essence. The symbol of the cow is common to Hetheru, Nut and Aset. The cow goddess is often referred to as a "seven fold deity" known as the "seven Hetherus" who preside over the life of each individual and the course of Creation. This title refers to the further differentiation of the three primordial principles of the Trinity (Asar-Aset-Heru) which is expressed as the phenomenal universe through a series of sevens. This number, *seven*, is expressed in all levels of Creation. It is expressed in the seven levels of the human subtle anatomy with the seven spiritual centers, and also as the seven primary colors of the rainbow. This principle of sevens translated into the Gnostic Idea of the "seven planetary spirits," and the Christian Archangels, known as the *Heads of the Celestial Host,* were titled the "Seven Archangels of the Presence."

Aset-Hetheru in Ancient Egypt symbolized the source of Creation. The *Milky Way* was produced by her udder and she was "the Great Cow which gave birth to Ra, the Great Goddess, the mother of all the gods and goddesses...the lady who existed when nothing else had being, and who created that which came into being." The cow is therefore a prominent representation of Aset and Hetheru. In her form as seven cows, Hetheru, an aspect of Aset, symbolizes the seven energies which course through the universe and which are sired by the *Bull* (Asar-male aspect of the Supreme Being). The *Bull* is a metaphor for the spirit. Just as the bull on a farm sires many cows, so to the "Bull" (Supreme Spirit) engenders all life in Creation.

In Indian Mythology, the cow holds a similar symbolism as that of Ancient Egypt. The cow is known as the "fountain of milk and curds." In a mystical sense, the world is a curd of the milk which emanated from the Celestial Cow (God). When the giant serpent of the Primeval Ocean moves, it churns the waters and thereby causes the waters to take on various shapes and forms just as churning milk causes it to turn into curds and butter. Curds are the part of milk that coagulates, i.e. goes from liquid to solid. The world is a curd in the ocean of consciousness, i.e. a coagulated thought of God, just as, when asleep, a dream is a coagulated manifestation of subconscious human desire.

In the mythology of Goddess Net it is explained that she gave birth to the Sundisk in her form as the Divine Cow. As she gave birth to the light she also gave birth to the darkness. Ra is that light and the darkness is his nemesis, the serpent demon Apep (Apophis of the Greek translation). Everyday Apep attempts to stop the voyage of the sun which is tantamount to attempting to stop Creation, for the voyage of Ra in his boat is what causes ripples in the primeval ocean. These ripples or more precisely, vibrations, cause the ocean to take on the form of waves. From the placid and inert state, matter has been transformed or conditioned. If this process stops Creation reverts back to its original undifferentiated state.

Picture 47: Set battles the Serpent Apep on behalf of Ra

This is why the goddess Maat sits at the bow (front) of the divine boat. She establishes order so that the boat may pass. In fact, Creation cannot function without order and this is the same order which keeps stars in their place, the sun in its course and the biological processes that sustain human life.

Picture 48: The Boat of Ra with Maat at the Bow

As Ra sails in his boat he establishes Maat (order) and sustains Creation. The figure below shows Ra in his boat with his daughter Maat sitting in the bow, breaking through the waters and thus making the way for him. Ra brought with him a Company of Gods and Goddesses, and through them (the neteru or cosmic forces of Creation, who are the primeval ocean itself), he manages Creation.

THE ASARIAN RESURRECTION

The Ausarian Resurrection myth was the most important one in all periods of Ancient Egyptian history and all of the other systems of theology had some relation it. According to tradition, Asar (Ausar, Asr - Osiris) and Ast (Aset - Isis) were the first King and Queen of Ancient Egypt. They taught the people agriculture, established a code of laws and taught all to worship the gods and goddesses as well as the Supreme Being, in the form of Ra. One version holds that one day, Asar's brother, Set, became jealous of Asar.

Set, who represents the personification of evil forces and negative qualities such anger, hatred and greed, plotted in jealousy and anger (the blinding passion that clouds the intellect) to usurp the throne and conspired to kill Osiris. Set secretly got the measurements of Osiris and constructed a coffin. Through trickery, Set was able to get Osiris to "try on" the coffin for size and while Osiris was resting in the coffin, Set and his assistants locked it and then dumped it into the Nile river.

The coffin made its way to the coast of Syria where it became embedded in the earth and from it grew a tree with the most pleasant aroma. The King of Syria was out walking and as he passed by the tree, he immediately fell in love with the pleasant aroma, so he had the tree cut down and brought to his palace and cut into the form of a DJED pillar. The Djed is the symbol of Osiris' BACK. It has four horizontal lines in relation to a firmly established, straight column. The DJED column is symbolic of the upper energy centers (chakras) that relate to the levels of consciousness of the spirit. Isis, Osiris' wife who is the personification of the life giving, mother force in creation and in all humans, went to Syria in search of Osiris. Her search led her to the palace of the Syrian King where she took a job as the nurse of the King's son. Isis then told the king that Osiris, her husband, is inside the pillar he made from the tree. The King graciously gave her the pillar and she returned with it to Kamit (Kmt, Ancient Egypt).

Upon her return to Kmt (Egypt), Isis went to the papyrus swamps where she lay over Osiris' dead body and conceived a son, Heru (Horus), through the spirit of Osiris with the assistance of the Gods Djehuti and Amun. One evening, as Set was hunting in the papyrus swamps, he came upon Isis, Osiris and the new born child. In a rage of passion, he dismembered the body of Osiris into fourteen pieces and scattered the pieces throughout the land. In this way, it is Set, the brute force of our bodily impulses and desires that "dismembers" our higher intellect. Under the influence of Set, instead of oneness and unity, we see multiplicity and separateness which give rise to egoistic (selfish) and violent behavior. Thus, the Ancient Egyptian character of Set is the prototype of the Jewish, Christian and Islamic "Satan." The Great Mother, Isis, once again set out to search, now for the pieces of Osiris, with the help of Apuat (Anubis) and Nebthet (Nephthys).

After searching all over the world, they found all of the pieces of Osiris' body, except for his phallus which was eaten by a fish. In Eastern Hindu-Tantra mythology, the God Shiva, who is the equivalent of Osiris, also lost his phallus by castration in one story. In Ancient Egyptian and Hindu-Tantra mythology, the loss represents seminal retention in order to channel the sexual energy to the higher spiritual centers, thereby transforming it into spiritual energy. In short, it represents cutting off of the desire for worldly pleasure in favor of spiritual realization. Isis, Anubis, and Nephthys "re-membered" all the pieces except the phallus which was eaten by a fish. Osiris thus, regained life in the realm of the dead. The sacred fish which ate the phallus of Osiris became the ritual fish of Christianity and one of the most popular symbols of Jesus.

Since Osiris was dead, Horus, therefore, was born from the union of the spirit of Osiris and the life giving power of Isis who represents supreme love and devotion to the Divine. In this manner, Osiris was resurrected and given life through the son, Horus, and becomes the God who presides over the fate of souls. Horus represents the union of spirit and matter, and the renewed life of Osiris, his rebirth or resurrection. When Horus became a young man, Osiris, in spirit form, encouraged him to take up arms (vitality, wisdom, courage, strength of will) and establish truth, justice and righteousness in the world by challenging Set, its current ruler. During the battle, Set injured the Eye of Horus (intuitional vision) and rendered him impotent against Set's powers (egoism, anger and hatred). Horus left the scene of the battle in order to contemplate his situation. Through the magic of right reasoning from Djehuti and the power of sexual sublimation from HetHeru (Hathor), Horus regained strength (spiritual energy, faith and will) to face Set again. Horus was able to wrest (gain control over) the testicles of Set and thus take away his power of brute force and egoistic impulsiveness. In achieving this control over Set, Horus was able to control the lower self and thereby allow his mind to operate unobstructed by the restless, agitated nature which comes from immaturity, emotionality and unbridled desires. The episode of Horus when he is injured and his subsequent time spent in solitude and reflection represents the stage of asceticism which implies celibacy and control over the senses in order to curb the externalized nature of the mind. The "battle" between Horus and Set is said to have lasted for three days. This is the same amount of time which was assigned to the resurrection of Jesus and to other saviors such as the god Attis.

Osiris represents the human soul. The soul is an emanation from the Divine and it incarnates in the realm of time and space and becomes intoxicated with the sense pleasures of creation. He is equivalent to the idea of Tem arising from the primeval waters after willing to evolve the universe and create order in the primeval chaotic waters. The lack of vigilance which caused his being tricked into the coffin of Set implies that Osiris forgot himself and allowed his passions to control him. This is the predicament of every soul who incarnates in the realm of time and space and forgets its primeval origin. However, Osiris is resurrected by righteousness, wisdom, devotion and supreme love, the qualities represented by Isis.

The term "chaotic" here refers to the primeval ocean. Originally it was formless and directionless. However, the movement of Ra causes waves in the ocean. Now the ocean is full of vibrations and motion. The ocean relates to pure consciousness like the mind when there are no thoughts. Also, this refers to the universe, the vastness of Creation which is involved with expansion and evolution out of the original rest and silence which was the primeval ocean. However, the more important reference relates to the mind and the state of consciousness wherein there is constant thinking and constant motion. Before Tem (Ra) emerges from the primeval waters there is calm and rest; there are no waves, no motion and no objectification (shapes or forms) of any kind in any part of the ocean. As soon as Tem emerges from the waters, however, there is objectification and separation of objects. The many waves ripple through the ocean creating many different looking images. Each wave creates a new image and different objects appear to exist within the ocean which was clear in the original calm state. Therefore, each object appears as being separate and distinct from the other.

This idea is inherent in the Ancient Egyptian Theban mythology concerning the god Amun and in the Memphite Theology concerning the god Ptah and it is equivalent to the Indian Vedantic teaching concerning Brahman and Narayana. As stated earlier, from a mystical point of view, this metaphor of the ocean refers to the mind. What is considered normal human consciousness is always in a state of motion due to thoughts. If those thoughts were to be somehow calmed, a new vision of reality would emerge in the mind which is not distorted by the wave-like thoughts. This attainment of a restful state of mind undisturbed by thoughts is achieved through the understanding of the myth and the practice of its teachings in day to day life along with meditation of the true nature of the soul.

Horus eventually regained rulership of Egypt and thereby redeemed his father. In so doing, Horus reestablished the correct position of the Divine (Osiris) and achieved control over the elements of the lower self as symbolized by Set (anger, hate, greed, lust, unrest, segmentation, etc.).

Re-membering the pieces of Osiris refers to the memory of the consciousness or the integration of the personality of the aspirant being re-integrated to a degree where the true self is discovered. An ordinary human being is not aware of his/her true nature because they are constantly in a state of worry, or preoccupation over some thought about the past, present or future. When the thoughts are recognized to be merely waves in the ocean of consciousness and the mind is calmed through the practice of yoga-wisdom and meditation, the mind assumes its unruffled state which then produces a clear image of the true self. This is the redemption and resurrection of our true self and it is the resurrection referred to by the Ausarian mystery and the Christian Gnostic mysticism. It does not refer to the resurrection of the physical body as asserted by the orthodox Roman theologians. It is, however, a resurrection in consciousness which is to occur while one is alive and existing in a physical body and not at some bodily resurrection at the end of time in some future *Armageddon.* The term Armageddon comes from the Hebrew term *har megiddo*, or "hill of Megiddo". In the Bible book of Revelation 16:16, the hill of Megiddo is the place where the final battle between the the forces of God and the demonic kings of the earth will be fought at the end of the world.

This remembrance is the main objective of the mystery rituals and practices in the religion of Osiris and Isis. Through the practice of Maat or virtuous actions and the constant remembrance of the divine essence of the individual self as being one with the Divine (Osiris) the aspirant is gradually led to identification with Osiris or the all-encompassing and transcendental Self. This process involves the identification of the aspirant with the Divine through ritual offerings to the Divine as the Self and to personal reference of the individual Self as the divine as well. In other words, the aspirant is treated as the Divinity, who has been dismembered and who is reconstituting him/her self in order to regain the primordial state of consciousness. The name of the aspirant is changed to Osiris as an understanding that the aspirant as all things, is a manifestation of the Divine Self. Since all is the Divine (Osiris), then all is to be named Osiris.

In the Ancient Egyptian Pyramid Texts, the entire subject of the rituals carried out by the aspirant involves accepting the ritual offerings of loaves of bread, cakes, wine, beer and other articles, which represent the *Eye* of intuitional vision. This Eye represents intuitional knowledge of the Self which is all powerful. The aspirant is continuously admonished to "receive" the Eye and to consume it as the essence of Horus and Osiris and to thereby assume his / her true nature in much the same way that the Christian "Host" is used as a medium to "Commune" with the Divine in the form of Christ. In this sense, the ritual of the Eucharist represents the open performance of the Ausarian mystery for the masses of Christians all over the world. However, is the true import of the ritual understood and practiced? The mystery play of the Ausarian Resurrection refers to a "mystical" re-enactment that relates to a mystical transformation that is to occur within the innermost heart of the individual as opposed to a ritual to be participated in out of custom or social duty. It is this mystical union with the Divine which bestows the true knowledge of the Self and it is this knowledge which the Sages of Ancient Egypt as well as their Gnostic descendants who created the Gnostic Christian gospels were trying to convey. This form of knowledge or Gnosticism is the mystical experience itself as opposed to the intellectual knowledge which can be found in scriptures or rituals. Therefore, it is this mystical experience of union with the Divine which is at the heart of all mystery religions and yoga philosophies.

In modern times, a philosophy called Agnosticism emerged. Agnosticism is a theory of religious understanding, associated with English rationalist Thomas Huxley (1825-95), who held that it is impossible either to demonstrate or to refute God's existence, on the basis of available evidence. This idea seems to discount the practice of rational introspection and the inquiry into the nature of matter (Quantum Physics) and the mystical experience (Yoga) as a real and viable method of discovering the Divine. This is a major problem for rational thinkers. They cannot look beyond logic and rationality in order to discover the transcendental nature of Creation so they stay within the confines of their mind and claim that there can be no proof or disproof of Divinity. Logic is like a double edged sword. If philosophy can show the falsehood of Creation it can also show the existence of Creation. This is why the scriptures hold that scriptures, wisdom teachings and logic are only roadmaps to the truth which is transcendental. This is why the deeper essence of spiritual teachings is not discovered by most people. They may be able to quote many scriptures, carry out elaborate rituals and so on but they do not practice the teachings and allow themselves to be transformed by them. For instance, the spiritual teachings of all the major religions are against killing but people in those religions kill every day. They kill people, animals, plants, insects, and themselves by smoking, eating meat, using drugs, etc. This is only a superficial practice of religion.

Through various arguments and similes, mystical philosophy shows that the phenomenal world is in reality an expression of the underlying divine essence. Modern physics would call this essence energy while mystical philosophy would call it consciousness. Nevertheless, philosophy is the discipline which trains the mind to become introspective and discerning of reality versus unreality. Mystical experience is the perfection and consummation of that practice and it is itself the proof of the Divine, transcendental state of consciousness. Therefore, those who refute the mysteries without undergoing the transformation from a conditioned state of mind will continue to remain oblivious to that which lies beyond the phenomenal world of time-space-causation which ordinary human consciousness is aware of exclusively.

The strong influence of the Ausarian Mystery was felt in later cults and mystery religions in the Near East under various names. Hippolitus quotes a Naasene source in the following: *"Hail Attis, gloomy mutilation of Rhea. Assyrians style thee thrice-longed-for Adonis, and the whole of Egypt calls thee Osiris,...; Samothracians, venerable Adam; Haemonians, Corybas; and the Phrygians named the at one time Pappa, at another time God... or the green Ear of Corn that has been reaped."*

Attis was a mystery religion imported into Rome around 204 B.C.E.. The Goddess *Cybele* begot Attis be eating an almond or pomegranate. Thus, she conceived Attis as a "virgin" as Isis had conceived Horus and as Mary would conceive Jesus. Attis's birthday is also on December 25th and his passion was celebrated on March 25, exactly nine months prior to the birthday on the winter solstice (like Jesus). Attis was a sacrificial victim who was slain and eaten in order to save humankind. He was eaten in the form of "bread" by his worshipers and he then resurrected as the "High God. The dates of Attis's death and resurrection are the same as those of Horus and later Jesus. Thus, the myths are synchronized as to the teaching concerning the resurrection of the soul since the passion and death is only a hint of the rebirth which will occur "nine months" later.

In mystical terms this passion play is referring to the ordinary unenlightened state of human consciousness which is led to repeated reincarnations only to experience countless births and deaths which include untold suffering and pain. The true aim of the mystery is for the initiate to assume the role of the victorious divinity and realize that she or he is in reality "The High Divinity" and to thereby end the cycle of births and deaths in order to resume the true state of being, free from the bonds of nature and ignorance.

Memphite Theology

The nature and composition of *"matter,"* or what is termed *"physical reality,"* and the concept of *"consciousness"* were understood and clearly set down in the hieroglyphic texts which date back to 5000 B.C.E in the theological system of Memphis, Egypt, as follows:

A-"Ptah conceived in his heart (reasoning consciousness) all that would exist and at his utterance (the word - will, power to make manifest), created Nun, the primeval waters (unformed matter-energy).

B- Then, not having a place to sit Ptah causes Nun to emerge from the primeval waters as the Primeval Hill so that he may have a place to sit. Atom then emerges and sits upon Ptah. Then came out of the waters four pairs of gods and goddesses, the Ogdoad (eight Gods):

C- Nun (primeval waters) and Nunet (heaven).
Huh (boundlessness) and Huhet (that which has boundaries).
Kuk (darkness) and Kuket (light).
Amon (the hidden) and Amonet (that which is manifest).

D- The Neteru (Nun, Nunet, Huh, Huhet, Kuk, Kuket, Amon, Amonet) are the lips and teeth of (God's) mouth which speaks the names of all things which come into existence . . .

E- . . The Heart and tongue have power over all the limbs. God is found as the heart within all bodies, and in the mouth of each neter and all humans as the tongue (will), of all things that live. . . It is God who thinks (as the Heart) and who commands (as the tongue). . .

F- . . . That which the nose breathes, the eyes see, the ears hear; all of these (senses) are communicated to the heart. It is the heart (mind) which makes all knowledge and awareness manifest, and then the tongue is what repeats what the heart has thought. . .

G- . . . All divine utterances manifested themselves through the thoughts of the heart and the commandments of the tongue. . .

H- . . . Justice is done to they who do what is loved, punishment to they who do what is hated. Life is given to they who are peaceful, death is given to the criminal. . .

I- ...In truth God (Ptah) caused the neteru to be born, the creation of the cities, establishment of the nomes, the establishment of the neteru in their places of adoration. . . God made their likenesses according to their desire. Thereby, the neteru entered into their bodies, the variety of wood, all types of mineral, clay, and all things that grow from these and in which they have taken place, foods, provisions, and all good things... He (Ptah) is Heru."

Thus, through the Shabaka Inscription, we are instructed in the following wisdom: **A:** Creation came into being through the mind (thought) of Ptah (the God of gods) and his utterance (power). **B-C-D:** Out of preexisting "Energy - Matter" (Nun), God then formed the principles by which they would be governed (four pairs of opposites). Atum or Tem performed the work of creation by sitting on Ptah, taking the creative thought, and then acting on the command of God. Therefore, the elements (matter) which constitute Creation, are the creative thought from God which "obey" God's will. GOD gives existence in the form of nature. **E-G:** Human consciousness and senses allow perception of and give meaning to that existence. God is conscious of creation, therefore, creation exists. What Gnosticism and Yoga philosophy term 'Universal Consciousness,' the "heart," is what modern physics would call "intelligence." This intelligence is the underlying reality behind all existence and all human experience. The senses receive the information from the environment and thereby register knowledge and existence. In fact, the world (creation) exists because consciousness (soul-intelligence) projects its existence through thought power just as a human mind projects the existence of a dream world during a dream. **H:** The law of Karma- cause and effect is establish to govern the entire creation. **I:** There can be no existence without consciousness to perceive it and sustain it. God (Ptah) IS the neteru and the Neteru are creation. Therefore, God and Creation are one and by understanding the creation and our own mind we can understand God and thus become one with God. Ptah and Heru, the Supreme Divinity of the Ausarian Resurrection, are one and the same. This shows synchronicity between these two Ancient Egyptian religions. They are not different but simply use different names to describe the divinities.

Neter Neteru
Nebertcher - Amun **(unseen, hidden, ever present, Supreme Being, beyond duality and description)**

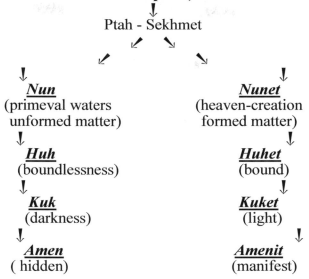

Ptah - Sekhmet

Nun (primeval waters unformed matter)	**_Nunet_** (heaven-creation formed matter)
Huh (boundlessness)	**_Huhet_** (bound)
Kuk (darkness)	**_Kuket_** (light)
Amen (hidden)	**_Amenit_** (manifest)

   The diagram above comes from Memphite Theology or the teaching that was espoused in the ancient Egyptian city of Het-Ka-Ptah (the Greek Memphis). It represents a development of the earlier themes presented in the Anunian creation teaching in reference to the attributes of the principles which have emanated from the Supreme Self, which go to constitute creation (pairs of opposites). The important idea to be understood here is that the origins of ancient Egypt are far off into the distant past. It is almost unimaginably ancient. However, there is something that surpasses even the great antiquity of ancient Egypt. The findings of modern science has shed light on the teachings of ancient Egypt and India. In both of these cosmological systems creation and time are understood in a circular way. This means that time moves in a circle rather than in a line from point A to point B as it is usually conceptualized in modern society. Modern science has shown that two lines moving in opposite directions join in infinity. This seems like a contradiction or paradox. However, upon reflection, the mystical wisdom of the ancients sheds light on this great truth.

A- The Ancient Egyptian Tree of Life of the Goddess, B- Christian Tree of Life. C Buddhist Tree of Life, D- Christian Christmas tree. E- The Caduceus of Djehuti (Hermes), F- The Psycho-spiritual Energy Centers of Serpent Power Yoga in Ancient Egypt and India.

(A)   (B)   (C)

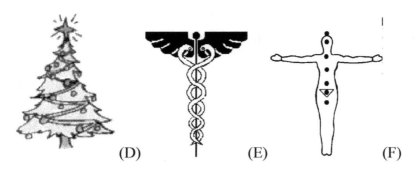

(D)   (E)   (F)

Kabbalism and its relation to Ancient Egypt

The Kabbalah (Cabbala) is an ancient sacred science of the study of Creation and man as developed by Jewish initiates. Its period of development spanned from the early Christian era to circa 1,200 A.C.E. The similarities to the Kemetic system are notable and thus merit mention here. Kabbalism constitutes the mystical branch of Judaism and is therefore compatible with Shetaut Neter (Ancient Egyptian Mysteries) in many ways. The similarities are further explained by the following. In the Bible, it is stated that Moses, who wrote the laws and guidelines for Jewish society, was knowledgeable in all of the wisdom and magic of Egypt; he was an Egyptian priest. The similarity between the 10 Commandments and the 42 Laws of Maat and the similarities with other scriptures will be noted upon simple comparison. The Tree of Life represents the ten aspects of Creation which in turn represent the ten aspects of GOD and the essence of the human soul. As in the Egyptian mystical system, the Kabbalah states that the tree of life is within the human being.

The tree corresponds to increasing levels of evolving consciousness and the Chakras or psychic energy centers. As in the Egyptian system of philosophy, if the various levels are explored and mastered, the human will know the true name and number of all that exists and have command of all the inner human forces (love, hate, greed, passion, etc.) and will know the names of spirits (Gods) and the seven forces (or powers). This is equal to the Egyptian teaching of achieving control over the Neters inside one's self and the doctrine of Hekau or words of power. Further, upon reaching the highest level, KETHER, which is equivalent to the Egyptian NETER, the human will attain cosmic consciousness and immortality. In the Kabalistic system, as well as the Egyptian, the same symbol for the Sun and Solar Life Force power is used: a dot surrounded by a circle:

Egyptian: Ra; Kabalistic: Tipheret

The Kabbalistic Mysticism of the Tree c. 1,200 A.C.E.

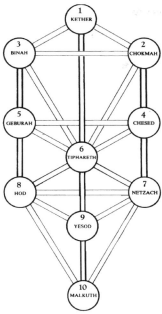

As in the Ancient Egyptian Mysticism related to the Pillar of Osiris, and the Tree of Anunian Theology, the discovery of the Kabbalistic *Tree of Life* in the Kabbalah is seen as the ultimate goal of life. The symbolism of the Kabbalistic tree of life is to be understood as a mystic code which holds the symbolism for the understanding of God and Creation as well as a mystic map showing the path to spiritual enlightenment. The Sefirotic Tree of Life consists of ten spiritual centers or Sefirofs which emanate from the Divine Self, God. These centers represent spiritual principles as well as psychological principles which need to be understood and mastered by the Kabbalistic aspirant in order to attain spiritual enlightenment at the top of the tree. It relates to the mystic symbolism of climbing up to heaven. The cross of Jesus is often referred to as a tree of life.

In the Bhagavad Gita of India (c.500 B.C.E.) the tree is used as a metaphor symbolizing that the world is not the source of its own existence but that indeed the Spirit is the source of Creation.

> 1. The Blessed Lord said: The scriptures speak of the imperishable Ashwattha tree (of the world-process) with its roots above and branches below; the Vedic verses constitute its leaves. He who knows this Tree is the knower of the essence of the Vedas.

Gita: Chapter 15

Purushottam Yogah--The Yoga of the Supreme Spirit

The same teaching is found in the Zohar text of Kabbalism, which reads: "The Tree of Life extends from above downwards, and is the sun, which illuminates all."

The philosophy of Kabbalism holds that the right side of the tree represents light and good and that the left side represents darkness or evil. This understanding is reminiscent of the Zoroastrian philosophy, which influenced early Judaism. Like Neberdjer of Ancient Egypt and Brahman of India, Kabbalism views God as Absolute and transcendental, *En-sof* (the infinite).

The Sefirot (spheres) are seen as attributes of God. As a human being develops these attributes they become godlike and therefore, Divine. The Spheres have been compared to the Chakras of Indian Kundalini Yoga and Ancient Egyptian Serpent Power mysticism. The meditations produce a similar mystical movement of energy (light and heat) in the subtle body of a human being which lead to greater experience of the Divine. When this form of ecstacy occurs it is called *shefa (divine influx)*. In contrast to the Serpent Power-kundalini Yoga system it is seen as an energy which comes into the body rather than lying dormant in it. As a human being masters the psycho-spiritual principle of the center he or she is able to move closer to the infinite. *Malkuth* represents the physical body, *Yesod* represents the *heart*, *Hod* represents the *Glory*, *Netzach* represents the *Victory*, *Tipthereth* represents the *Intellect*, *Geburah* represents the *Force*, *Chesed* represents the *Mercy*, *Binah* represents the *Wisdom*, *Chokmah* represents the *Light*, and Kether represents the *spirit* and *humility*. The lower seven spheres have been related to the seven psycho-spiritual consciousness energy of the subtle spine (Serpent Power, Kundalini Yoga). The three upper spheres are explained as mystical steps towards unity with God. Thus, through meditation and contemplation on the tree an aspirant climbs up through the principles of life and Creation.

The *Sefer Yezirah* or Kabbalistic "Book of Creation" says that God created the universe through thirty-two paths of wisdom. These are represented by the ten sephirot and the twenty-two letters of the Hebrew alphabet. The sephirot originally represented numbers and later came to be interpreted as emanations from which all existence originates and has its basis.

On the Following page: Representation of the Anunian Tree of Gods and Goddesses (Pautti).

The Tree of Life of Pharaonic Theology

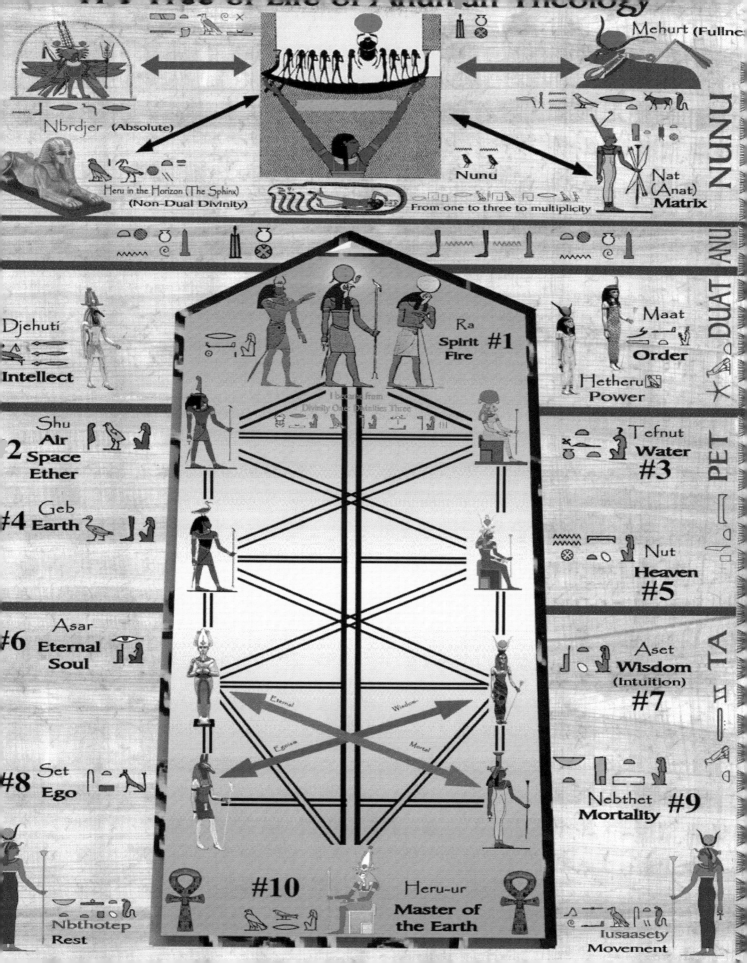

Nbrdjer (Absolute)

Heru in the Horizon (The Sphinx)
(Non-Dual Divinity)

Nunu

From one to three to multiplicity

Mehurt (Fullne...

Nat (Anat)
Matrix

NUNU

ANU

DUAT

PET

TA

Djehuti
Intellect

Ra
Spirit Fire #1

Maat
Order

Hetheru
Power

Shu
**Air
Space
Ether** #2

Tefnut
Water #3

#4 Geb
Earth

Nut
Heaven #5

#6 Asar
**Eternal
Soul**

Aset
Wisdom
(Intuition) #7

#8 Set
Ego

Nebthet
Mortality #9

I became from
Divinity One, Divinities Three

Eternal   Wisdom

Egoism   Mortal

#10   Heru-ur
**Master of
the Earth**

Nbthotep
Rest

Iusaasety
Movement

The Mysticism of the Ancient Egyptian Pautti and Its Relation to the Sefirotic Tree of Life of the Kabbalah

It is clear to see that the exposition of the *Sefirotic Tree of Life* in the Kabbalah expresses the understanding of Creation as an emanation from that which is subtle (the spirit) to that which is gross (the earth). A brief overview of the Ancient Egyptian Pautti or Company of Gods and Goddesses of Creation, provides insights into the deeper teachings intimated in the Kabbalistic tree mysticism. The Sefer Yezirah is actually a scripture of cosmology and cosmogony which attempts to explain the nature, structure and substance of Creation. The Ancient Egyptian Creation myth also attempts to explain the nature of Creation. The extraordinary factor about the Ancient Egyptian Creation myth is that it achieves the same teaching but not through spheres but through *Neteru* or god and goddess principles.

CONCLUSION

Out of ignorance of the deeper Self, most people (the masses) are caught between the dualistic thoughts of their mind. They have not discovered the transcendental peace, so therefore they are caught up in the waves of positive and negative emotions and the desires for acquiring something which they perceive will bring happiness. Ignorant people live life in a state of delusion. There is a constant belief that the world will somehow bring them happiness, despite the relentless disappointments and frustrations. It is like gambling. There is a constant expectation that one will win, even though the odds are stacked against it. Even if there is a win, it is not really a win because the winnings will be used to strengthen the belief in the world and will set up the winner for an even bigger disappointment later on. Spiritual life does not mean that there is no fun or experience of pleasure due to objects of the world. It means that there is no dependence on the world for happiness, instead there is indifference. If pleasure is experienced a Sage accepts it. If pleasure is not experienced a Sage also accepts this. At no time does the absence or presence of pleasure due to worldly objects or situations affect the deeper experience of peace and joy which comes from the inner Self. Therefore, the experiences of pleasure and pain remain in the enlightened state but they are transcended with the ever-present knowledge of the innermost Self within. It is like standing on the shore and looking at the ocean. Even though the different waves are there the ocean cannot be missed. Likewise a Sage looks at the pain and sorrow of life as waves but never looses sight of the Self which surges like an ocean in every corner of Creation. Thus, the abiding presence of wisdom and Divine awareness in the mind overpowers all disturbances of the outside world even as those movements, changes, sounds, situations, the passage of time, emotions, waking, dream, dreamless sleep, etc. may continue. For the enlightened Sage these waves are seen as transient forms which will pass as they give way to new ones. So there is no mourning over, attachment to or leaning upon the past or the future nor for anything that is fleeting, uncertain and unstable. Of course, the Sage harbors no desire or longings for anything that is not real and abiding and so experiences constant peace, contentment and bliss internally even while carrying out the various duties of life or even while performing the most dynamic work in the service of humanity. The ability to sidestep the pitfalls of human existence in the form of anger, hatred, greed, pain, sorrow, lack of egoistic desires, etc. allows a Sage to conserve energy and to attune the mind to the heavenly realms where it is possible to gain intuitive communion with the Higher Self (God) and, in so doing, bring the marvels of spiritual wisdom to humanity through literary works, and teaching humanity through various means which require a high degree of stamina and resiliency. This is the art of living which a

Sage lives by and which he or she teaches to others for the purpose of leading them to spiritual realization and to promote peace and harmony in the world.

Those who are Enlightened and have come to understand their oneness with Osiris go to rejoin Osiris in the *Beautiful West* (the Land of the Setting Sun- Ra), also known as Amenta, and become one with him. When you succeed in cultivating an intuitive intellect (*Saa*) which understands the nature of creation and the oneness of all things in the one "Hidden God," then you will achieve *Saa-Amenti-Ra,* the intelligence or knowledge of the Amenti of Ra, the hidden world. Those who do not achieve this level of spiritual realization are subjected to the various experiences which can occur in the Duat. Notice that the teaching of the Duat incorporates the main characters of the Ancient Egyptian religion: Amun, Ra and Osiris, thus showing the uniformity of its understanding and the synchronicity of its teaching throughout Ancient Egypt.

How to Practice Anunian Theology

Creation is a task in which the spirit, Ra, engages on a moment by moment basis. If the Spirit ceased to sustain Creation even for a moment all nature would revert back to its primordial form, the Nun. In the same manner a spiritual aspirant needs to engage in continuous spiritual disciplines. In this manner, their movement towards enlightenment and immortality is assured. Otherwise, even dedicated aspirants can fail in "sustaining" a viable and successful life and success in their spiritual lives.

The practice of Anunian Theology involves the study of the wisdom teachings related to Anunian Theology, discovering the mythic origins of Creation. Then it is necessary to practice the rituals related to the teachings of Anunian Theology which involves the disciplines of mystic spirituality (Chanting the Divine name, reciting hymns related to Ra and his children, acting with Maat (righteousness), performing the rituals of the solar worship (daily three-fold worship- at dawn, noon and dusk, facing the sun in the east, north and west, respectively) and Uaa (meditation) on the Akhu nature of Self. The reader is advised to study the following books, which expand on the teachings of Anunian Theology. Those books are ***The Glorious Light Meditation System, Resurrecting Osiris, The Egyptian Yoga Daily Chant and Songbook*** and ***The Book of the Dead,*** all of which are available through C.M. Books (see back Section). This manner of study, along with listening to taped lectures by Dr. Muata Ashby, expounding on the philosophy contained in the teachings, allows a spiritual aspirant to gain insight into the higher mystical philosophy that is contained therein. Through this process an aspirant is led to discover higher and higher consciousness until there is a realization of oneness with the Ra-Akhu or Spirit of Ra. This is called ***Enlightenment, Self-Knowledge, Nirvana, Resurrection, Liberation, immortality, etc.***

Dua Ra, Dua Ra, Dua Ra Khepera!
Adorations to Ra, Adorations to Ra,
Adorations to Ra in the form of Khepera!

Index

Abdu, 26

Absolute, 16, 31, 32, 49, 62, 66, 81, 83, 90, 132, 138, 153

Absolute XE "Absolute" Reality, 83

Acts, 132

Adonis, 149

Africa, 3, 7, 8, 15, 36, 175

African Religion, 175

Air, 82

Akhemu Seku, 116

Akhemu Urdu, 116

Akhenaton, 129, 131, 132, 133

Akher, 98, 99, 113

Akhnaton, 27

Akhus, 30

Allah, 32, 134

Amen, 58, 75, 131, 142, 151

Amenta, 58, 72, 157, 171

Amentet, 116, 142, 173

Amun, 14, 18, 21, 24, 31, 47, 48, 55, 58, 59, 60, 61, 62, 64, 85, 87, 89, 96, 120, 127, 131, 133, 134, 135, 136, 140, 143, 146, 147, 151, 157

Amun-Ra-Ptah, 31, 47, 48, 60, 85, 133, 135

Ancient Egypt, 1, 3, 7, 8, 10, 15, 16, 17, 19, 31, 33, 36, 41, 45, 47, 48, 50, 51, 53, 56, 57, 60, 61, 62, 64, 65, 66, 69, 74, 76, 77, 82, 83, 84, 87, 89, 90, 91, 93, 94, 95, 97, 98, 100, 101, 102, 103, 104, 108, 114, 116, 118, 123, 124, 125, 127, 129, 131, 132, 133, 134, 136, 137, 141, 144, 145, 146, 147, 148, 150, 151, 152, 153, 154, 156, 157, 167, 168, 169, 170, 171, 172, 173, 174, 175, 176, 177, 178, 179

Ancient Egyptian Mystical Philosophy, 83

Ancient Egyptian Pyramid Texts, 82, 116, 148

Ani, 59, 127, 128

Ankh, 124

Anpu, 80

Anu, 1, 9, 14, 21, 22, 33, 45, 47, 61, 66, 87, 88, 93, 94, 97, 102, 104, 119, 120, 133, 172

Anu (Greek Heliopolis), 1, 9, 14, 21, 22, 33, 45, 47, 61, 66, 87, 88, 93, 94, 97, 102, 104, 119, 120, 133, 172

Anubis, 40, 41, 46, 48, 67, 80, 146

Anunian Theology, 18, 21, 22, 33, 62, 63, 71, 81, 84, 93, 96, 100, 125, 129, 133, 153, 158

Apep serpent, 29, 72, 126, 144

Apophis, 29, 144

Architecture, 108

Ari, 14

Armageddon, 147

Aryan, 10, 169

Asar, 14, 18, 21, 22, 26, 31, 35, 36, 37, 39, 40, 41, 44, 45, 47, 67, 75, 76, 78, 79, 80, 81, 82, 83, 85, 87, 88, 89, 90, 91, 93, 95, 97, 100, 112, 116, 117, 119, 123, 124, 125, 126, 127, 131, 134, 135, 136, 141, 143, 144, 145, 171, 173, 178, 179

Asarian Resurrection, 18, 87, 171, 173, 174, 175

Asclepius, 116

Aset, 7, 8, 18, 22, 25, 26, 35, 36, 39, 40, 41, 42, 44, 45, 47, 50, 67, 74, 76, 78, 79, 81, 82, 83, 87, 88, 89, 91, 93, 100, 117, 119, 123, 125, 134, 135, 136, 137, 141, 143, 144, 145, 169, 171, 173, 178

Aset (Isis), 7, 8, 18, 22, 25, 26, 35, 36, 39, 40, 41, 42, 44, 45, 47, 50, 67, 74, 76, 78, 79, 81, 82, 83, 87, 88, 89, 91, 93, 100, 117, 119, 123, 125, 134, 135, 136, 137, 141, 143, 144, 145, 169, 171, 173, 178

Assyrians, 149

Astral, 107, 125, 127, 171

Astral Plane, 107, 125, 127, 171

Aten, see also Aton, 126, 129, 132, 179

Atlantis, 176

Atom, 51, 149

Aton, 14, 21, 27, 129, 131, 132

Atonism, 27, 129, 131

Attis, 146, 149

Atum, 47, 49, 51, 75, 87, 88, 89, 90, 91, 93, 96, 97, 98, 99, 100, 119, 150

Balance, 74

Being, 13, 16, 17, 19, 20, 21, 34, 47, 48, 49, 60, 62, 75, 83, 87, 109, 110, 120, 123, 126, 127, 130, 134, 135, 143, 144, 172

Benben, 34, 93, 94, 108

Bhagavad Gita, 53, 56, 153

Other Books From C M Books

P.O.Box 570459
Miami, Florida, 33257
(305) 378-6253 Fax: (305) 378-6253

This book is part of a series on the study and practice of Ancient Egyptian Yoga and Mystical Spirituality based on the writings of Dr. Muata Abhaya Ashby. They are also part of the Egyptian Yoga Course provided by the Sema Institute of Yoga. Below you will find a listing of the other books in this series. For more information send for the Egyptian Yoga Book-Audio-Video Catalog or the Egyptian Yoga Course Catalog.

Now you can study the teachings of Egyptian and Indian Yoga wisdom and Spirituality with the Egyptian Yoga Mystical Spirituality Series. The Egyptian Yoga Series takes you through the Initiation process and lead you to understand the mysteries of the soul and the Divine and to attain the highest goal of life: ENLIGHTENMENT. The *Egyptian Yoga Series*, takes you on an in depth study of Ancient Egyptian mythology and their inner mystical meaning. Each Book is prepared for the serious student of the mystical sciences and provides a study of the teachings along with exercises, assignments and projects to make the teachings understood and effective in real life. The Series is part of the Egyptian Yoga course but may be purchased even if you are not taking the course. The series is ideal for study groups.

Prices subject to change.

1. EGYPTIAN YOGA: THE PHILOSOPHY OF ENLIGHTENMENT An original, fully illustrated work, including hieroglyphs, detailing the meaning of the Egyptian mysteries, tantric yoga, psycho-spiritual and physical exercises. Egyptian Yoga is a guide to the practice of the highest spiritual philosophy which leads to absolute freedom from human misery and to immortality. It is well known by scholars that Egyptian philosophy is the basis of Western and Middle Eastern religious philosophies such as *Christianity, Islam, Judaism,* the *Kabala,* and Greek philosophy, but what about Indian philosophy, Yoga and Taoism? What were the original teachings? How can they be practiced today? What is the source of pain and suffering in the world and what is the solution? Discover the deepest mysteries of the mind and universe within and outside of your self. 8.5" X 11" ISBN: 1-884564-01-1 Soft $19.95

2. EGYPTIAN YOGA II: The Supreme Wisdom of Enlightenment by Dr. Muata Ashby ISBN 1-884564-39-9 $23.95 U.S. In this long awaited sequel to *Egyptian Yoga: The Philosophy of Enlightenment* you will take a fascinating and enlightening journey back in time and discover the teachings which constituted the epitome of Ancient Egyptian spiritual wisdom. What are the disciplines which lead to the fulfillment of all desires? Delve into the three states of consciousness (waking, dream and deep sleep) and the fourth state which transcends them all, Neberdjer, "The Absolute." These teachings of the city of Waset (Thebes) were the crowning achievement of the Sages of Ancient Egypt. They establish the standard mystical keys for understanding the profound mystical symbolism of the Triad of human consciousness.

3.   THE KEMETIC DIET: GUIDE TO HEALTH, DIET AND FASTING Health issues have
always been important to human beings since the beginning of time. The earliest records
of history show that the art of healing was held in high esteem since the time of Ancient
Egypt. In the early 20th century, medical doctors had almost attained the status of
sainthood by the promotion of the idea that they alone were "scientists" while other
healing modalities and traditional healers who did not follow the "scientific method' were
nothing but superstitious, ignorant charlatans who at best would take the money of their
clients and at worst kill them with the unscientific "snake oils" and "irrational theories".
In the late 20th century, the failure of the modern medical establishment's ability to lead
the general public to good health, promoted the move by many in society towards
"alternative medicine". Alternative medicine disciplines are those healing modalities
which do not adhere to the philosophy of allopathic medicine. Allopathic medicine is
what medical doctors practice by an large. It is the theory that disease is caused by
agencies outside the body such as bacteria, viruses or physical means which affect the
body. These can therefore be treated by medicines and therapies The natural healing
method began in the absence of extensive technologies with the idea that all the answers
for health may be found in nature or rather, the deviation from nature. Therefore, the
health of the body can be restored by correcting the aberration and thereby restoring
balance. This is the area that will be covered in this volume. Allopathic techniques have
their place in the art of healing. However, we should not forget that the body is a grand
achievement of the spirit and built into it is the capacity to maintain itself and heal itself.
Ashby, Muata ISBN: 1-884564-49-6 $28.95

4.   INITIATION INTO EGYPTIAN YOGA Shedy: Spiritual discipline or program, to go
deeply into the mysteries, to study the mystery teachings and literature profoundly, to
penetrate the mysteries. You will learn about the mysteries of initiation into the teachings
and practice of Yoga and how to become an Initiate of the mystical sciences. This
insightful manual is the first in a series which introduces you to the goals of daily
spiritual and yoga practices: Meditation, Diet, Words of Power and the ancient wisdom
teachings. 8.5" X 11" ISBN 1-884564-02-X   Soft Cover $24.95 U.S.

5.   *THE AFRICAN ORIGINS OF CIVILIZATION, MYSTICAL RELIGION AND YOGA
PHILOSOPHY* HARD COVER EDITION ISBN: 1-884564-50-X $80.00 U.S.   81/2"
X 11"   Part 1, Part 2, Part 3 in one volume 683 Pages Hard Cover First Edition Three
volumes in one. Over the past several years I have been asked to put together in one
volume the most important evidences showing the correlations and common teachings
between Kamitan (Ancient Egyptian) culture and religion and that of India. The questions
of the history of Ancient Egypt, and the latest archeological evidences showing
civilization and culture in Ancient Egypt and its spread to other countries, has intrigued
many scholars as well as mystics over the years. Also, the possibility that Ancient
Egyptian Priests and Priestesses migrated to Greece, India and other countries to carry on
the traditions of the Ancient Egyptian Mysteries, has been speculated over the years as
well. In chapter 1 of the book *Egyptian Yoga The Philosophy of Enlightenment*, 1995, I
first introduced the deepest comparison between Ancient Egypt and India that had been
brought forth up to that time. Now, in the year 2001 this new book, *THE AFRICAN
ORIGINS OF CIVILIZATION, MYSTICAL RELIGION AND YOGA PHILOSOPHY,* more

fully explores the motifs, symbols and philosophical correlations between Ancient Egyptian and Indian mysticism and clearly shows not only that Ancient Egypt and India were connected culturally but also spiritually. How does this knowledge help the spiritual aspirant? This discovery has great importance for the Yogis and mystics who follow the philosophy of Ancient Egypt and the mysticism of India. It means that India has a longer history and heritage than was previously understood. It shows that the mysteries of Ancient Egypt were essentially a yoga tradition which did not die but rather developed into the modern day systems of Yoga technology of India. It further shows that African culture developed Yoga Mysticism earlier than any other civilization in history. All of this expands our understanding of the unity of culture and the deep legacy of Yoga, which stretches into the distant past, beyond the Indus Valley civilization, the earliest known high culture in India as well as the Vedic tradition of Aryan culture. Therefore, Yoga culture and mysticism is the oldest known tradition of spiritual development and Indian mysticism is an extension of the Ancient Egyptian mysticism. By understanding the legacy which Ancient Egypt gave to India the mysticism of India is better understood and by comprehending the heritage of Indian Yoga, which is rooted in Ancient Egypt the Mysticism of Ancient Egypt is also better understood. This expanded understanding allows us to prove the underlying kinship of humanity, through the common symbols, motifs and philosophies which are not disparate and confusing teachings but in reality expressions of the same study of truth through metaphysics and mystical realization of Self. (HARD COVER)

6.   AFRICAN ORIGINS BOOK 1 PART 1 African Origins of African Civilization, Religion, Yoga Mysticism and Ethics Philosophy-Soft Cover $24.95 ISBN: 1-884564-55-0

7.   AFRICAN ORIGINS BOOK 2 PART 2 African Origins of Western Civilization, Religion and Philosophy(Soft) -Soft Cover $24.95 ISBN: 1-884564-56-9

8.   EGYPT AND INDIA (AFRICAN ORIGINS BOOK 3 PART 3) African Origins of Eastern Civilization, Religion, Yoga Mysticism and Philosophy-Soft Cover $29.95 (Soft) ISBN: 1-884564-57-7

9.   THE MYSTERIES OF ISIS: **The Ancient Egyptian Philosophy of Self-Realization** - There are several paths to discover the Divine and the mysteries of the higher Self. This volume details the mystery teachings of the goddess Aset (Isis) from Ancient Egypt- the path of wisdom. It includes the teachings of her temple and the disciplines that are enjoined for the initiates of the temple of Aset as they were given in ancient times. Also, this book includes the teachings of the main myths of Aset that lead a human being to spiritual enlightenment and immortality. Through the study of ancient myth and the illumination of initiatic understanding the idea of God is expanded from the mythological comprehension to the metaphysical. Then this metaphysical understanding is related to you, the student, so as to begin understanding your true divine nature. ISBN 1-884564-24-0 $22.99

10.   EGYPTIAN PROVERBS: TEMT TCHAAS *Temt Tchaas* means: collection of ——
Ancient Egyptian Proverbs How to live according to MAAT Philosophy. Beginning
Meditation. All proverbs are indexed for easy searches. For the first time in one volume,
——Ancient Egyptian Proverbs, wisdom teachings and meditations, fully illustrated with
hieroglyphic text and symbols. EGYPTIAN PROVERBS is a unique collection of
knowledge and wisdom which you can put into practice today and transform your life.
5.5"x 8.5" $14.95 U.S   ISBN: 1-884564-00-3

11.   THE PATH OF DIVINE LOVE The Process of Mystical Transformation and The Path
of Divine Love   This Volume focuses on the ancient wisdom teachings of "Neter
Merri" –the Ancient Egyptian philosophy of Divine Love and how to use them in a
scientific process for self-transformation. Love is one of the most powerful human
emotions. It is also the source of Divine feeling that unifies God and the individual
human being. When love is fragmented and diminished by egoism the Divine connection
is lost. The Ancient tradition of Neter Merri leads human beings back to their Divine
connection, allowing them to discover their innate glorious self that is actually Divine
and immortal. This volume will detail the process of transformation from ordinary
consciousness to cosmic consciousness through the integrated practice of the teachings
and the path of Devotional Love toward the Divine. 5.5"x 8.5" ISBN 1-884564-11-9
$22.99

12.   INTRODUCTION TO MAAT PHILOSOPHY: Spiritual Enlightenment Through the
Path of Virtue   Known as Karma Yoga in India, the teachings of MAAT for living
virtuously and with orderly wisdom are explained and the student is to begin practicing
the precepts of Maat in daily life so as to promote the process of purification of the heart
in preparation for the judgment of the soul. This judgment will be understood not as an
event that will occur at the time of death but as an event that occurs continuously, at
every moment in the life of the individual. The student will learn how to become allied
with the forces of the Higher Self and to thereby begin cleansing the mind (heart) of
impurities so as to attain a higher vision of reality. ISBN 1-884564-20-8 $22.99

13.   MEDITATION The Ancient Egyptian Path to Enlightenment   Many people do not
know about the rich history of meditation practice in Ancient Egypt. This volume
outlines the theory of meditation and presents the Ancient Egyptian Hieroglyphic text
which give instruction as to the nature of the mind and its three modes of expression. It
also presents the texts which give instruction on the practice of meditation for spiritual
Enlightenment and unity with the Divine. This volume allows the reader to begin
practicing meditation by explaining, in easy to understand terms, the simplest form of
meditation and working up to the most advanced form which was practiced in ancient
times and which is still practiced by yogis around the world in modern times. ISBN 1-
884564-27-7 $24.99

14.   THE GLORIOUS LIGHT MEDITATION Technique of Ancient Egypt ISBN: 1-
884564-15-1$14.95 (PB) New for the year 2000. This volume is based on the earliest
known instruction in history given for the practice of formal meditation. Discovered by
Dr. Muata Ashby, it is inscribed on the walls of the Tomb of Seti I in Thebes Egypt. This

volume details the philosophy and practice of this unique system of meditation originated in Ancient Egypt and the earliest practice of meditation known in the world which occurred in the most advanced African Culture.

15. THE SERPENT POWER: The Ancient Egyptian Mystical Wisdom of the Inner Life Force.   This Volume specifically deals with the latent life Force energy of the universe and in the human body, its control and sublimation. How to develop the Life Force energy of the subtle body. This Volume will introduce the esoteric wisdom of the science of how virtuous living acts in a subtle and mysterious way to cleanse the latent psychic energy conduits and vortices of the spiritual body. ISBN 1-884564-19-4 $22.95

16. EGYPTIAN YOGA *The Postures of The Gods and Goddesses* Discover the physical postures and exercises practiced thousands of years ago in Ancient Egypt which are today known as Yoga exercises. This work is based on the pictures and teachings from the Creation story of Ra, The Asarian Resurrection Myth and the carvings and reliefs from various Temples in Ancient Egypt 8.5" X 11" ISBN 1-884564-10-0 Soft Cover $21.95 Exercise video $20

17. EGYPTIAN TANTRA YOGA: The Art of Sex Sublimation and Universal Consciousness This Volume will expand on the male and female principles within the human body and in the universe and further detail the sublimation of sexual energy into spiritual energy. The student will study the deities Min and Hathor, Asar and Aset, Geb and Nut and discover the mystical implications for a practical spiritual discipline. This Volume will also focus on the Tantric aspects of Ancient Egyptian and Indian mysticism, the purpose of sex and the mystical teachings of sexual sublimation which lead to self-knowledge and Enlightenment. 5.5"x 8.5" ISBN 1-884564-03-8 $24.95

18. ASARIAN RELIGION: RESURRECTING OSIRIS The path of Mystical Awakening and the Keys to Immortality NEW REVISED AND EXPANDED EDITION!   The Ancient Sages created stories based on human and superhuman beings whose struggles, aspirations, needs and desires ultimately lead them to discover their true Self. The myth of Aset, Asar and Heru is no exception in this area. While there is no one source where the entire story may be found, pieces of it are inscribed in various ancient Temples walls, tombs, steles and papyri. For the first time available, the complete myth of Asar, Aset and Heru has been compiled from original Ancient Egyptian, Greek and Coptic Texts. This epic myth has been richly illustrated with reliefs from the Temple of Heru at Edfu, the Temple of Aset at Philae, the Temple of Asar at Abydos, the Temple of Hathor at Denderah and various papyri, inscriptions and reliefs. Discover the myth which inspired the teachings of the *Shetaut Neter* (Egyptian Mystery System - Egyptian Yoga) and the Egyptian Book of Coming Forth By Day. Also, discover the three levels of Ancient Egyptian Religion, how to understand the mysteries of the Duat or Astral World and how to discover the abode of the Supreme in the Amenta, *The Other World*   The ancient religion of Asar, Aset and Heru, if properly understood, contains all of the elements necessary to lead the sincere aspirant to attain immortality through inner self-discovery. This volume presents the entire myth and explores the main mystical themes and rituals associated with the myth for understating human existence, creation and the way to

achieve spiritual emancipation - *Resurrection.* The Asarian myth is so powerful that it influenced and is still having an effect on the major world religions. Discover the origins and mystical meaning of the Christian Trinity, the Eucharist ritual and the ancient origin of the birthday of Jesus Christ. Soft Cover ISBN: 1-884564-27-5 $24.95

19. **THE EGYPTIAN BOOK OF THE DEAD MYSTICISM OF THE PERT EM HERU** $28.95   ISBN# 1-884564-28-3 Size: 8½" X 11" I Know myself, I know myself, I am One With God!–From the Pert Em Heru "The Ru Pert em Heru" or "Ancient Egyptian Book of The Dead," or "Book of Coming Forth By Day" as it is more popularly known, has fascinated the world since the successful translation of Ancient Egyptian hieroglyphic scripture over 150 years ago. The astonishing writings in it reveal that the Ancient Egyptians believed in life after death and in an ultimate destiny to discover the Divine. The elegance and aesthetic beauty of the hieroglyphic text itself has inspired many see it as an art form in and of itself. But is there more to it than that? Did the Ancient Egyptian wisdom contain more than just aphorisms and hopes of eternal life beyond death? In this volume Dr. Muata Ashby, the author of over 25 books on Ancient Egyptian Yoga Philosophy has produced a new translation of the original texts which uncovers a mystical teaching underlying the sayings and rituals instituted by the Ancient Egyptian Sages and Saints. "Once the philosophy of Ancient Egypt is understood as a mystical tradition instead of as a religion or primitive mythology, it reveals its secrets which if practiced today will lead anyone to discover the glory of spiritual self-discovery. The Pert em Heru is in every way comparable to the Indian Upanishads or the Tibetan Book of the Dead." Muata Abhaya Ashby

20. **ANUNIAN THEOLOGY THE MYSTERIES OF RA** The Philosophy of Anu and The Mystical Teachings of The Ancient Egyptian Creation Myth Discover the mystical teachings contained in the Creation Myth and the gods and goddesses who brought creation and human beings into existence. The Creation Myth holds the key to understanding the universe and for attaining spiritual Enlightenment. ISBN: 1-884564-38-0 40 pages $14.95

21. **MYSTERIES OF MIND** Mystical Psychology & Mental Health for Enlightenment and Immortality based on the Ancient Egyptian Philosophy of Menefer -Mysticism of Ptah, Egyptian Physics and Yoga Metaphysics and the Hidden properties of Matter.   This volume uncovers the mystical psychology of the Ancient Egyptian wisdom teachings centering on the philosophy of the Ancient Egyptian city of Menefer (Memphite Theology). How to understand the mind and how to control the senses and lead the mind to health, clarity and mystical self-discovery. This Volume will also go deeper into the philosophy of God as creation and will explore the concepts of modern science and how they correlate with ancient teachings. This Volume will lay the ground work for the understanding of the philosophy of universal consciousness and the initiatic/yogic insight into who or what is God? ISBN 1-884564-07-0 $22.95

22. **THE GODDESS AND THE EGYPTIAN MYSTERIESTHE PATH OF THE GODDESS THE GODDESS PATH** The Secret Forms of the Goddess and the Rituals of Resurrection The Supreme Being may be worshipped as father or as mother. *Ushet Rekhat* or *Mother*

Worship, is the spiritual process of worshipping the Divine in the form of the Divine Goddess. It celebrates the most important forms of the Goddess including *Nathor, Maat, Aset, Arat, Amentet and Hathor* and explores their mystical meaning as well as the rising of *Sirius,* the star of Aset (Aset) and the new birth of Hor (Heru). The end of the year is a time of reckoning, reflection and engendering a new or renewed positive movement toward attaining spiritual Enlightenment. The Mother Worship devotional meditation ritual, performed on five days during the month of December and on New Year's Eve, is based on the Ushet Rekhit. During the ceremony, the cosmic forces, symbolized by Sirius - and the constellation of Orion ---, are harnessed through the understanding and devotional attitude of the participant. This propitiation draws the light of wisdom and health to all those who share in the ritual, leading to prosperity and wisdom. $14.95 ISBN 1-884564-18-6

23.   *THE MYSTICAL JOURNEY FROM JESUS TO CHRIST* $24.95   ISBN# 1-884564-05-4 size: 8½" X 11" Discover the ancient Egyptian origins of Christianity before the Catholic Church and learn the mystical teachings given by Jesus to assist all humanity in becoming Christlike. Discover the secret meaning of the Gospels that were discovered in Egypt. Also discover how and why so many Christian churches came into being. Discover that the Bible still holds the keys to mystical realization even though its original writings were changed by the church. Discover how to practice the original teachings of Christianity which leads to the Kingdom of Heaven.

24.   THE STORY OF ASAR, ASET AND HERU: An Ancient Egyptian Legend (For Children)   Now for the first time, the most ancient myth of Ancient Egypt comes alive for children. Inspired by the books *The Asarian Resurrection: The Ancient Egyptian Bible* and *The Mystical Teachings of The Asarian Resurrection, The Story of Asar, Aset and Heru* is an easy to understand and thrilling tale which inspired the children of Ancient Egypt to aspire to greatness and righteousness.   If you and your child have enjoyed stories like *The Lion King* and *Star Wars you will love The Story of Asar, Aset and Heru.* Also, if you know the story of Jesus and Krishna you will discover than Ancient Egypt had a similar myth and that this myth carries important spiritual teachings for living a fruitful and fulfilling life. This book may be used along with *The Parents Guide To The Asarian Resurrection Myth: How to Teach Yourself and Your Child the Principles of Universal Mystical Religion.* The guide provides some background to the Asarian Resurrection myth and it also gives insight into the mystical teachings contained in it which you may introduce to your child. It is designed for parents who wish to grow spiritually with their children and it serves as an introduction for those who would like to study the Asarian Resurrection Myth in depth and to practice its teachings. 41 pages 8.5" X 11"   ISBN: 1-884564-31-3 $12.95

25.   THE PARENTS GUIDE TO THE AUSARIAN RESURRECTION MYTH: How to Teach Yourself and Your Child the Principles of Universal Mystical Religion.   This insightful manual brings for the timeless wisdom of the ancient through the Ancient Egyptian myth of Asar, Aset and Heru and the mystical teachings contained in it for parents who want to guide their children to understand and practice the teachings of mystical spirituality. This manual may be used with the children's storybook *The Story of*

Asar, Aset and Heru by Dr. Muata Abhaya Ashby. 5.5"x 8.5"   ISBN: 1-884564-30-5 $14.95

26.   HEALING THE CRIMINAL HEART BOOK 1 Introduction to Maat Philosophy, Yoga and Spiritual Redemption Through the Path of Virtue   Who is a criminal? Is there such a thing as a criminal heart? What is the source of evil and sinfulness and is there any way to rise above it? Is there redemption for those who have committed sins, even the worst crimes?   Ancient Egyptian mystical psychology holds important answers to these questions. Over ten thousand years ago mystical psychologists, the Sages of Ancient Egypt, studied and charted the human mind and spirit and laid out a path which will lead to spiritual redemption, prosperity and Enlightenment.   This introductory volume brings forth the teachings of the Asarian Resurrection, the most important myth of Ancient Egypt, with relation to the faults of human existence: anger, hatred, greed, lust, animosity, discontent, ignorance, egoism jealousy, bitterness, and a myriad of psycho-spiritual ailments which keep a human being in a state of negativity and adversity. 5.5"x 8.5"   ISBN: 1-884564-17-8 $15.95

27.   THEATER & DRAMA OF THE ANCIENT EGYPTIAN MYSTERIES: Featuring the Ancient Egyptian stage play-"The Enlightenment of Hathor' Based on an Ancient Egyptian Drama, The original Theater -Mysticism of the Temple of Hetheru $14.95 By Dr. Muata Ashby

28.   GUIDE TO PRINT ON DEMAND: SELF-PUBLISH FOR PROFIT, SPIRITUAL FULFILLMENT AND SERVICE TO HUMANITY Everyone asks us how we produced so many books in such a short time. Here are the secrets to writing and producing books that uplift humanity and how to get them printed for a fraction of the regular cost. Anyone can become an author even if they have limited funds. All that is necessary is the willingness to learn how the printing and book business work and the desire to follow the special instructions given here for preparing your manuscript format. Then you take your work directly to the non-traditional companies who can produce your books for less than the traditional book printer can. ISBN: 1-884564-40-2 $16.95 U. S.

29.   Egyptian Mysteries: Vol. 1, Shetaut Neter ISBN: 1-884564-41-0 $19.99 What are the Mysteries? For thousands of years the spiritual tradition of Ancient Egypt, *Shetaut Neter,* "The Egyptian Mysteries," "The Secret Teachings," have fascinated, tantalized and amazed the world. At one time exalted and recognized as the highest culture of the world, by Africans, Europeans, Asiatics, Hindus, Buddhists and other cultures of the ancient world, in time it was shunned by the emerging orthodox world religions. Its temples desecrated, its philosophy maligned, its tradition spurned, its philosophy dormant in the mystical *Medu Neter,* the mysterious hieroglyphic texts which hold the secret symbolic meaning that has scarcely been discerned up to now. What are the secrets of *Nehast* {spiritual awakening and emancipation, resurrection}. More than just a literal translation, this volume is for awakening to the secret code *Shetitu* of the teaching which was not deciphered by Egyptologists, nor could be understood by ordinary spiritualists. This book is a reinstatement of the original science made available for our times, to the reincarnated followers of Ancient Egyptian culture and the prospect of spiritual freedom to break the bonds of *Khemn,* "ignorance," and slavery to evil forces: *Såaa* .

30. EGYPTIAN MYSTERIES VOL 2: Dictionary of Gods and Goddesses ISBN: 1-884564-23-2 $21.95 This book is about the mystery of neteru, the gods and goddesses of Ancient Egypt (Kamit, Kemet). Neteru means "Gods and Goddesses." But the Neterian teaching of Neteru represents more than the usual limited modern day concept of "divinities" or "spirits." The Neteru of Kamit are also metaphors, cosmic principles and vehicles for the enlightening teachings of Shetaut Neter (Ancient Egyptian-African Religion). Actually they are the elements for one of the most advanced systems of spirituality ever conceived in human history. Understanding the concept of neteru provides a firm basis for spiritual evolution and the pathway for viable culture, peace on earth and a healthy human society.   Why is it important to have gods and goddesses in our lives? In order for spiritual evolution to be possible, once a human being has accepted that there is existence after death and there is a transcendental being who exists beyond time and space knowledge, human beings need a connection to that which transcends the ordinary experience of human life in time and space and a means to understand the transcendental reality beyond the mundane reality.

31. EGYPTIAN MYSTERIES VOL. 3 The Priests and Priestesses of Ancient Egypt ISBN: 1-884564-53-4 $22.95 This volume details the path of Neterian priesthood, the joys, challenges and rewards of advanced Neterian life, the teachings that allowed the priests and priestesses to manage the most long lived civilization in human history and how that path can be adopted today; for those who want to tread the path of the Clergy of Shetaut Neter.

32. THE KING OF EGYPT: The Struggle of Good and Evil for Control of the World and The Human Soul ISBN 1-8840564-44-5 $18.95   This volume contains a novelized version of the Asarian Resurrection myth that is based on the actual scriptures presented in the Book Asarian Religion (old name –Resurrecting Osiris). This volume is prepared in the form of a screenplay and can be easily adapted to be used as a stage play. Spiritual seeking is a mythic journey that has many emotional highs and lows, ecstasies and depressions, victories and frustrations. This is the War of Life that is played out in the myth as the struggle of Heru and Set and those are mythic characters that represent the human Higher and Lower self. How to understand the war and emerge victorious in the journey o life? The ultimate victory and fulfillment can be experienced, which is not changeable or lost in time. The purpose of myth is to convey the wisdom of life through the story of divinities who show the way to overcome the challenges and foibles of life. In this volume the feelings and emotions of the characters of the myth have been highlighted to show the deeply rich texture of the Ancient Egyptian myth. This myth contains deep spiritual teachings and insights into the nature of self, of God and the mysteries of life and the means to discover the true meaning of life and thereby achieve the true purpose of life. To become victorious in the battle of life means to become the King (or Queen) of Egypt.Have you seen movies like The Lion King, Hamlet, The Odyssey, or The Little Buddha? These have been some of the most popular movies in modern times. The Sema Institute of Yoga is dedicated to researching and presenting the wisdom and culture of ancient Africa. The Script is designed to be produced as a motion

picture but may be addapted for the theater as well. $19.95   copyright 1998 By Dr. Muata Ashby

33.   AFRICAN DIONYSUS: FROM EGYPT TO GREECE: The Kamitan Origins of Greek Culture and Religion ISBN: 1-884564-47-X $24.95 U.S. FROM EGYPT TO GREECE This insightful manual is a reference to Ancient Egyptian mythology and philosophy and its correlation to what later became known as Greek and Rome mythology and philosophy. It outlines the basic tenets of the mythologies and shoes the ancient origins of Greek culture in Ancient Egypt. This volume also documents the origins of the Greek alphabet in Egypt as well as Greek religion, myth and philosophy of the gods and goddesses from Egypt from the myth of Atlantis and archaic period with the Minoans to the Classical period. This volume also acts as a resource for Colleges students who would like to set up fraternities and sororities based on the original Ancient Egyptian principles of Sheti and Maat philosophy. ISBN: 1-884564-47-X $22.95 U.S.

34.   THE FORTY TWO PRECEPTS OF MAAT, THE PHILOSOPHY OF RIGHTEOUS ACTION AND THE ANCIENT EGYPTIAN WISDOM TEXTS ADVANCED STUDIES This manual is designed for use with the 1998 Maat Philosophy Class conducted by Dr. Muata Ashby. This is a detailed study of Maat Philosophy. It contains a compilation of the 42 laws or precepts of Maat and the corresponding principles which they represent along with the teachings of the ancient Egyptian Sages relating to each. Maat philosophy was the basis of Ancient Egyptian society and government as well as the heart of Ancient Egyptian myth and spirituality. Maat is at once a goddess, a cosmic force and a living social doctrine, which promotes social harmony and thereby paves the way for spiritual evolution in all levels of society. ISBN: 1-884564-48-8 $16.95 U.S.

Music Based on the Prt M Hru and other Kemetic Texts

Available on Compact Disc $14.99 and Audio Cassette $9.99

Adorations to the Goddess

Music for Worship of the Goddess

NEW Egyptian Yoga Music CD
by Sehu Maa
Ancient Egyptian Music CD
Instrumental Music played on reproductions of Ancient Egyptian Instruments– Ideal for <u>meditation</u> and
reflection on the Divine and for the practice of spiritual programs and <u>Yoga exercise sessions.</u>

©1999 By Muata Ashby
CD $14.99 –

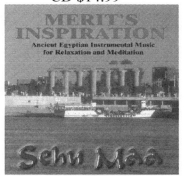

MERIT'S INSPIRATION
NEW Egyptian Yoga Music CD
by Sehu Maa
Ancient Egyptian Music CD
Instrumental Music played on
reproductions of Ancient Egyptian Instruments– Ideal for <u>meditation</u> and
reflection on the Divine and for the practice of spiritual programs and <u>Yoga exercise sessions.</u>
©1999 By
Muata Ashby
CD $14.99 –
UPC# 761527100429

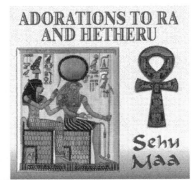

ANORATIONS TO RA AND HETHERU
NEW Egyptian Yoga Music CD
By Sehu Maa (Muata Ashby)
Based on the Words of Power of Ra and HetHeru
played on reproductions of Ancient Egyptian Instruments **Ancient Egyptian Instruments used: Voice, Clapping, Nefer Lute, Tar Drum, Sistrums, Cymbals** – The Chants, Devotions, Rhythms and Festive Songs Of the Neteru – Ideal for meditation, and devotional singing and dancing.

©1999 By Muata Ashby
CD $14.99 –
UPC# 761527100221

SONGS TO ASAR ASET AND HERU
NEW
Egyptian Yoga Music CD
By Sehu Maa
played on reproductions of Ancient Egyptian Instruments– The Chants, Devotions, Rhythms and Festive Songs Of the Neteru - Ideal for meditation, and devotional singing and dancing.
Based on the Words of Power of Asar (Asar), Aset (Aset) and Heru (Heru) Om Asar Aset Heru is the third in a series of musical explorations of the Kemetic (Ancient Egyptian) tradition of music. Its ideas are based on the Ancient Egyptian Religion of Asar, Aset and Heru and it is designed for listening, meditation and worship. ©1999 By Muata Ashby
CD $14.99 –
UPC# 761527100122

HAARI OM: ANCIENT EGYPT MEETS INDIA IN MUSIC
NEW Music CD
By Sehu Maa

The Chants, Devotions, Rhythms and
Festive Songs Of the Ancient Egypt and India, harmonized and played on reproductions of ancient instruments along with modern instruments and beats. Ideal for meditation, and devotional singing and dancing.
Haari Om is the fourth in a series of musical explorations of the Kemetic (Ancient Egyptian) and Indian traditions of music, chanting and devotional spiritual practice. Its ideas are based on the Ancient Egyptian Yoga spirituality and Indian Yoga spirituality.
©1999 By Muata Ashby
CD $14.99 –
UPC# 761527100528

RA AKHU: THE GLORIOUS LIGHT
NEW
Egyptian Yoga Music CD
By Sehu Maa
The fifth collection of original music compositions based on the Teachings and Words of The Trinity, the God Asar and the Goddess Nebethet, the Divinity Aten, the God Heru, and the Special Meditation Hekau or Words of Power of Ra from the Ancient Egyptian Tomb of Seti I and more...
played on reproductions of Ancient Egyptian Instruments and modern instruments - **Ancient Egyptian Instruments used: Voice, Clapping, Nefer Lute, Tar Drum, Sistrums, Cymbals**
– The Chants, Devotions, Rhythms and Festive Songs Of the Neteru – Ideal for meditation, and devotional singing and dancing.
©1999 By Muata Ashby
CD $14.99 –

UPC# 761527100825

GLORIES OF THE DIVINE MOTHER
Based on the hieroglyphic text of the worship of Goddess Net.
The Glories of The Great Mother
©2000 Muata Ashby
CD $14.99 UPC# 761527101129`

Order Form

Telephone orders: Call Toll Free: 1(305) 378-6253. Have your AMEX, Optima, Visa or MasterCard ready.

   Fax orders: 1-(305) 378-6253 E-MAIL ADDRESS: Semayoga@aol.com

Postal Orders: Sema Institute of Yoga, P.O. Box 570459, Miami, Fl. 33257. USA.

Please send the following books and / or tapes.

ITEM

_____Cost $_____

_____Cost $_____

_____Cost $_____

_____Cost $_____

_____Cost $_____

            Total $_____

Name:_____

Physical Address:_____

City:_____ State:_____ Zip:_____

Sales tax: Please add 6.5% for books shipped to Florida addresses

_____Shipping: $6.50 for first book and .50¢ for each additional

_____Shipping: Outside US $5.00 for first book and $3.00 for each additional

_____Payment:_____

_____Check -Include Driver License #:

  _____

_____Credit card: _____ Visa, _____ MasterCard, _____ Optima,

_____ AMEX.

Card number:_____

Name on card:_____ Exp. date:_____/_____

Copyright 1995-2005 Dr. R. Muata Abhaya Ashby

Sema Institute of Yoga

P.O.Box 570459, Miami, Florida, 33257

(305) 378-6253 Fax: (305) 378-6253

---

[i] i am follower of Neberdjer... *Pert M Heru* Chap 4 (commonly 17)

[ii] The Supreme Being, all-encompassing Divinity